the
singer's
art

THE SINGER'S ART

An Analysis Of Vocal Principles

BY

Richard DeYoung
MUS.D.

PUBLISHED BY

DePaul University

CHICAGO

Distributed by
North Shore Press
535 South Sheridan Road
Waukegan, Illinois

The Author Gratefully Acknowledges the Professional Assistance of Mme. Claire Dux and the Editorial Assistance of Dr. Norman Sigband, Mr. Hugh Walpole, and Miss Barbara Gilbert

CONTENTS

FOREWORD

By Claire Dux, former opera star and symphony soloist. Famous singer of Mozart and Schubert. Grand niece of Robert Schumann and personal friend of Richard Strauss.

PAGE XIII

INTRODUCTION

A note to the teacher; a word to the student.

PAGE XVI

Chapter 1. CHOOSING YOUR GOAL

What success really is. Its ingredients and requirements.

PAGE 21

Chapter 2. CHARTING YOUR COURSE

A singer's plan and the mental disciplines required.

PAGE 33

Chapter 3. HOW A SINGER BREATHES

The physiological and psychological elements of breath control.

PAGE 42

Chapter 4. THE TONE BEGINS—RESONANCE

The structure of the voice. The physiological aspects of phonation and its by-products, resonance, range and volume.

PAGE 53

Chapter 5. ARTICULATION

The vowel as an essential element in diction and in vocal technique. The way to open the mouth. The relation of consonants to the tone

IX

line and clear enunciation. The attainment of linguistic facility.

PAGE 63

Chapter 6. PHONETICS
The sounds of syllables as distinguished from their spellings. The phonetic symbols illustrated by examples.

PAGE 74

Chapter 7. REGISTERS
The key to the even scale and adequate range. A mystery explained.

PAGE 78

Chapter 8. FLEXIBILITY AND AGILITY
Flexibility as response to feeling indicated by volume changes and sensitivity. Agility as facility and accuracy as execution of music.

PAGE 88

Chapter 9. INTERFERENCES AND THEIR CORRECTION
Compensatory efforts and their causes.

PAGE 94

Chapter 10. TRAINING THE YOUNG VOICE
The importance of early impressions and basic habits. The changing boy voice.

PAGE 101

Chapter 11. VOCAL HEALTH
A review of physical conditions and what influences them. The various problems of throat conditions. The dangers of vocal abuse and of self-treatment of infections. The influence of smoking, alcohol and environment on the voice.

PAGE 107

Chapter 12. MUSICIANSHIP
The key to accuracy of intonation and the devices of musical expression or interpretation.

PAGE 118

Chapter 13. SONG STYLES
The study of song sources and their treatment.
PAGE 125

Chapter 14. INTERPRETATION
The art of performance detailed. The singer's communication with the public.
PAGE 134

Chapter 15. TONE COLOR
The place of emotion in public performance. Inspiration as a communicative or a destructive force.
PAGE 142

Chapter 16. PERSONALITY
A light touch upon a tremendously important subject.
PAGE 145

Chapter 17. THE PSYCHOLOGICAL ASPECT OF SUCCESS
The various aspects of the singer's thinking. Mental order and direction. The use of memory, concentration, appreciation and cultural consideration.
PAGE 153

Chapter 18. THE CAREER
When, where and how singing may be made a life work.
PAGE 161

XI

Claire Dux was one of the finest Mozart singers of her time. So great was her fame in Europe that she was made honorary president of the Mozart Gemeinde which built and now maintains the Mozarteum in Salzburg. She was equally renowned as a concert artist and sang in all the capitals of Europe as well as the major cities of the United States.

Sir Thomas Beecham, when visiting Chicago, made the following statement: "Once, years ago, I was looking for a dramatic lyric soprano for the leading role in Mozart's opera, The Magic Flute. But a light soprano, in the part, sounds like a child soloist forlornly chanting in a great cathedral.

"I could find no voice that suited me, and said so to composer Richard Strauss. But he said, 'There is a young singer with our Berlin Opera company who could do the role for you. Come and hear her,' he urged me.

"I did hear her. And she sang more than 300 performances of The Magic Flute under my direction. Chaliapin, Melba, Caruso, and other great artists came to sit in the front row and applaud whenever she appeared. It is due to her that I am in Chicago. For that young singer was Claire Dux, now Mrs. Hans von Der Marwitz."

After ten years at the Staatsoper in Berlin she was engaged by the Chicago Opera Company and the N.B.C. Concert Service. While on tour for N.B.C. Concert Service, she was given an honorary music doctorate by the University of Southern California. She has been an ardent patron of the arts in Chicago. An intimate friend of Dr. Frederick A. Stock, she did much to help bring the Chicago Symphony Orchestra to its present eminence.

FOREWORD
By Claire Dux

"Every book worth reading is a meeting place. Some would call it a battleground: are the writer's ideas or the reader's preconceptions to survive?" Thus the eminent literary critic I. A. Richards begins his introduction to a book on semantics: and truly any useful book must indeed provide for a meeting of minds. Here Mr. De Young opens hospitable doors to young American singers and their teachers. This book combines statements of scientific facts, viewpoints on methods of thinking, and expositions on philosophies of life as they relate to the singer and to the teacher of singing.

Today much responsibility for the singer's development falls upon himself. In our society, aspiring singing artists do not have the opportunity for guidance and supervision which were provided in the seventeenth century by the Papal School at Rome. Those singers practiced and were trained to a perfection that ever since has been the envy of the singing world.

Today there are undoubtedly more trained

XIII

singers than ever before. In the singer's education emphasis is increasingly falling upon his responsibility to study and guide his own progress.

Mr. De Young stresses very well the importance of the way in which the singer thinks. Ultimately the learning process takes place *in his consciousness*. His mind must guide him as a performer and as an instrument, for the singer is unique in playing that dual musical role.

It is well that in the United States so much progress has been made in organizing teachers of singing and helping them to realize, as a corporate body, so to speak, the essential part they have to play in this country's culture. All such efforts must help to create higher standards and bring about long-needed improvements in their backgrounds of training. Association with their colleagues will surely help to make teachers aware of their strengths and weaknesses in musical knowledge, musical sensitivity, and in the vital task of sympathizing with and understanding the personalities of the students they must guide.

Mr. De Young reminds us of the multitude of young men and women who begin a singing career, but how few persevere and finally succeed in reaching the goal of finished public artists. There are many reasons for this. For the singer, intelligence and character are even more important than his vocal gifts. In addition he must have good training, he must discipline himself, and he must be technically accurate and perfect.

It is fashionable in some artistic circles to put what I consider far too much emphasis upon a singer's "personality." If you have this magic personality, some say, you will reach the heights regardless of defects in technique. But it works the other way about: the person who does all the work and achieves all the necessary growth to become a consummate artist automatically is a personality. Granted this persistent training and technical proficiency, the singer's career stands or falls upon a succession of personal victories over needs and obstacles. Kipling's "If" is now passé, and never was a good poem, but it does hint at the depths of spirit on which the singer must school himself to rely. When you are a singer you have to do a thing right many times in practice until you convince your inner self that you can accomplish it perfectly whenever called upon.

The dedicated musician must keep his eye constantly on his goal while cultivating the mastery of techniques and the mental and emotional maturity his public expects.

These generalizations apply to any profession or pursuit, but musicians will know that they apply particularly to us; exactly how and why we are clearly and emphatically told in this book. In the field of singing, the artist can never finish learning. The best athletes receive continual expert coaching even when they attain supremacy in their chosen sport. So too the singer requires the constant direction and counsel of a singing instructor throughout his career.

Mr. De Young's career as singer and teacher goes back almost half a century. Besides his own work, he has spent his energies working for the entire profession. One of the founders of the National Association of Teachers of Singing, and a past president of that organization, he works at present as an active member of its Vocal Education Committee. His whole career, and this book itself, provide good testimony that he is qualified to write it.

Claire Dux

XV

INTRODUCTION

Success in singing can be realized by anyone who has vocal and musical talent, a better than average intelligence and the willingness to work hard. The formula is not the same for any two people. To know which course he should follow the singer must consult somebody who knows the field of music intimately, someone who can lead and inform, somebody who can judge and inspire him. These pages do not constitute an instruction book; rather are they indicators of direction, or milestones along the way.

He must have a clearly pictured goal. This goal should be a standard of excellence rather than a place or a time. Where he sings, for whom, what kind of music—these will be determined by the course his development takes.

Success bears so many different labels and comes in packages of such varying size that it cannot be outlined. Success in singing could attend any one of a dozen or more separate occupations. But one qualification marks them all: *you must excel*. There is no room at the top for mediocrity. Whether the goal be opera, television, show business or the concert stage, it still requires a victorious person with singleness of purpose who never gives up or loses his way.

The singer will surely appreciate that no book can replace his own work or that of his teacher. Perhaps he does some teaching himself, in which case he knows what a marvel of virtuosity a teacher of singing must try to be. A teacher should be a master musician. Besides being well grounded in the science of acoustics, he must have a keen and efficient ear to discriminate qualities of sound, gradations of volume, and phonetic accuracy. He must know how to train you so that your actual performance is perfectly coordinated with your mental concept. He must be physiologist enough to act as vocal therapist, by himself or in consultation with a medical specialist, when such care is needed. He must be your advisor both pedagogically and as a psychologist. He must be all these and much more, and no book can take his place.

Critics and others who write about music often complain that those learning or teaching how to sing seem to have no norm, no standard practice. Some class subjects can be generalized, and taught to large groups at one time. But singing is the creative act of a single individual. No two human beings are alike. We think, choose and express ourselves individually. The successful path that one artist follows may not prove as rewarding for another. A teacher would no more train two students in the same manner than a doctor would treat two patients alike. The remedy and the program of action depend upon the individual diagnosis.

Beautiful singing demands obedience to the

laws of nature, musical accuracy and spontaneous creative feeling. The teacher and the singer must know all the scientific principles involved in the singing act, plus a thorough knowledge of music and linguistics. But all these are but means towards the full release of the artist's emotional and creative energies.

Our universe is individualized. No two leaves on a tree are alike. Of the millions of people on earth no two have the same finger prints. Why then expect anything as individual as singing to follow a fixed pattern? With instrumentalists it is different. They may play the same piano or the same violin. But the singer is *himself* his instrument. His physical equipment is his healthy body, and his voice is a mental concept—an image, a sense of vocal sound.

Nobody can disobey the laws of natural science and sing well. Nobody can disobey his country's laws and be a good citizen. But making one's full contribution to society involves much more than merely observing laws, and becoming a good singer demands much more than the following of a few basic principles.

There are techniques that govern any act requiring both knowledge and skill, whether it be surgery or singing. In the pages which follow, the reader will find descriptions of the techniques that apply to singing. The development of these techniques is the mutually shared task of the teacher and the singer. To specify these techniques in detail would be asking the reader to adopt the method and approach of some individual teacher, or some one singing artist. This brief work is not such an attempt. It may provoke questions and differences of opinion. Such discussion is salutory and welcome.

XVIII

The following chapters are road signs. They give directions; real success will come from within the singer himself. He alone must travel every inch of the way.

CHOOSING YOUR GOAL

Generations of singers have proved that success in the singing field still requires what it did in the days of Patti, Schumann-Heink and Caruso—excellence in musicianship, vocal capacity and a communicative personality. It makes very little difference in which field of music one wishes to make public contact; the emphasis varies but the key remains the same. One must *excel* in his chosen field, and he must possess the equipment and development that that field demands.

MASS PRODUCTION AND OPPORTUNITY

It is not true, as so many believe, that modern conditions, with music performed by mass media, have reduced the opportunities for a successful career. As with all other technological progress, the greater availability of music has made careers possible in more diversified fields than ever before. More people listen to music than in any time in history. Some seek it as entertainment and diversion, while many more recognize it as emotional and spiritual stimulation and as a mark

21

of culture and refined taste.

The true artist is still in great demand. Increasingly intelligent discrimination expects expertness whether in public performance or in teaching, and this applies to any area of musical expression.

Expertness is based upon experience, and experience is the sum total of all that has gone before. This is sometimes referred to as "the hard way" as if there were some other way. The public is sometimes dazzled and gullible enough to think that the possession of a marked talent is sufficient. They forget, or they never hear of the importance of long hard years of study and apprenticeship, or of the services of expensive press agents who cleverly build up publicity regarding some recent "discovery."

Famous, well known artists in the operatic, concert and entertainment fields tell the same story. Grace Moore's background is typical. She began her career in a night club in Greenwich Village, then on to a Broadway review for two or three seasons. After extended study in Europe, she made her debut there. Finally, after years of work and study Miss Moore became a star with the Metropolitan Opera.

INGREDIENTS OF SUCCESS

What, then, are the ingredients of lasting success in the singing field? Naturally, a marked talent comes first. A singer must possess the material for success before it can come out. How can he know if he has it? He must seek sound, honest advice. If a healthy voice, sensitive musical perception, and a gift for expression through words are in evidence, then the intensity of the desire will tell him.

Desire must be the unquenchable fire that keeps the boilers hot and the steam up. The power of application, the zest for work, the courage to overcome impatience, disappointment, delay and all types of frustration depend on the power the boiler generates. A love of beauty, particularly for music, a deep wish to accomplish, to become a victorious soul, no matter what the cost—these constitute the first ingredient, *desire*.

Singing and Teaching Require Health

A healthy body comes next. A singer or a teacher must be durable. From a physical standpoint, singing is a functional act, and it follows that all functions must be adequate. A sense of well-being, buoyant health and an alert mind can easily become a habit. Those who cultivate it are fortunate. But there are many who are perfectly healthy whose dread of contracting a disease or becoming ill is so constant that they attract such conditions. Negative attitudes like this have prevented many people from fully enjoying and using the good health they have.

Necessary Musical Talent

Next we might place the gift of musicality. Musicality is a sensitive appreciation for values in sound. Recognition of pitch, quality, volume, and color in sound are really what "having a voice" means. Most people have healthy throats and are amply energetic, but singing requires a sense of musical values before a healthy mechanism can be called a good voice. On the other hand musicianship is the result of education and training, and this education needs innate musicality as its base.

An instinct for expression should be considered

23

next in the review of the ingredients for success in singing.

Human beings communicate with one another in many ways, but the most familiar vehicle is language. Personality is often reflected by the language the singer uses; the expression of the word; the presentation of the phrase. The word and its place in the singer's equipment are described in greater length in Chapter Five.

Finally a Personality

An attractive personality is the art of communication in its most manifest form. All the artist's attitudes toward himself, his work and people unite to constitute his manner of address. His background of education and culture, his philosophy of life, even when instinctive instead of consciously chosen, are evident in the quality and character of expression we call personality. Magnetism is another matter and its degree is something with which we are born, but personality is an ever growing, ever expanding thing, feeding on experience, encouragement and ever increasing confidence.

All these elements, when adequate, make intimate or direct communication possible.

PURPOSE

The careers of other artists often serve as inspiration and guidance for us, if we will but study them. Grace Moore, an American artist whom we mentioned earlier in this chapter can serve as an illustration. She had humble beginnings, but she became so great a star in grand opera, stage, moving pictures and radio that her name became a household word, not only in her own country, but all over the world.

24

Singing always came first with her. The wish to sing and be popular were always passionate desires. From her youthful days in high school, Miss Moore always knew just what she wanted, and she lived with a singleness of purpose that never swerved from the desired goal. Reading her autobiography *You Are Only Human Once,* which she attempts to make light and entertaining, you will learn of some of the obstacles that temporarily blocked her path, and also some of her lucky "breaks." Whatever else one may say about Grace Moore, and there are many who still remember her, she had indomitable courage. This combination—the definite goal and the tremendous desire to win—could well be called the two basic ingredients of success.

Mr. J. Sig Paulson has written,

"The most important element in successful happy living is *singleness of purpose.* This is true in any field, whether it be business, politics, or one of the professions. Take a close look at the successful, happy men and women you have met or seen or hear, and you will find that they have one quality in common—purpose. They have a goal that they want to attain in life. Their sights are trained on an objective to which they are willing to devote their strength, their means, their thinking, their faith, their enthusiasm, their talents and their abilities. They gladly give up certain pleasures, which may seem highly important to others; they will even endure seeming hardships and inconveniences in order to further the purpose to which their lives are dedicated.

A little observation will disclose that failure and frustration have a common denominator—lack of purpose. The individual who admits failure is really saying that he does not have a purpose big enough to make him willing to keep trying, and to keep working to overcome whatever obstacles may seem to be in the way of his success. True purpose does not recognize failure as having finality. Success or failure is not dependent on the number and size of obstacles, but on the sincerity and intensity of one's purpose. Real purpose calls forth the wisdom, strength and energy needed for its own fulfillment.

There are countless geniuses buried in the ruts of mediocrity simply because they have never found a purpose in life that would focus and give direction to their talents and abilities."

The first thing I am going to advise is that the singer get his ambition as clear in his mind as he can. The more concretely he pictures his goal at the start, the better will be his chance of holding on to the road and reaching his destination. There are four main goals for the singer. They are not incompatible but the young singer must decide their order of importance for himself. Otherwise, he is in danger of being rather in the predicament of that fabulous donkey that starved because it was halfway between two stacks of hay, and never managed to make up its mind which to choose.

Is money the chief goal? There is lots of money to be made by singing in both the classical and popular music business. He will need to become somewhat wordly in matters of making contacts, getting publicity, keeping a sharp eye open to lucrative fields, as well as giving attention to the development of that *degree of excellence* the field demands.

Is it fame he wants? Most of us long sometimes to have our pictures in all the papers, and our names in blazing lights in the world's biggest cities. The desire for prominence is a healthy kind of exhibitionism that keeps many a useful citizen working through all discouragement.

Does he aim for proficiency in the art of singing and musical accomplishment? He is fortunate if he genuinely loves music, and is willing to achieve success through this patient and persevering way.

The fourth goal I have in mind is that of creative personal satisfaction. He is doing what he wants to do, studying an art that is far greater than any of us, and doing his best to become a worthy performer. I think of many past students as I speak of this. Many of them made sacrifices to keep up their singing. Some singers who aim at this goal already have professions or careers in which they are economically successful; but their inner needs still urge them towards music. I think also of persons who have worked away year after year for the pleasure of keeping their minds quick and keen, of learning how to handle themselves well in public and the joy of learning new material.

Naturally, the student will discuss these matters with a teacher, but the essential decision is his own. When he has decided what he is going to do, he will probably have to be rather "hard-boiled" in persevering in his purposes and in studying the "angles" of what in many of its aspects is a severe field of endeavor.

WHAT IS SUCCESS

In these days the achievement of fame has become what one might call a technical science. Entertainment celebrities pay their publicity agents high salaries to get and keep them on the front page. All sorts of devices are used to gain public attention and sympathy. Many an incident, which has seemed a fortuitous circumstance, has been carefully thought out and planned beforehand. In the entertainment field one rarely becomes a "name singer" just because he can sing. There is usually some other reason. Fan clubs are an advantage, if he is a man, for the teen-age swooners are generally girls. But to sell a million records, or to appear on a television show once a week he must have something, be it acting talent, good looks, voice or personality. He must have some *plus* quality over and above his musical gifts and training.

He may become famous in some fields without making a great deal of money. A dramatic soprano I knew sang in an opera company, was guest soloist a few times on radio programs, appeared occasionally with symphony orchestras or oratorio societies, but never made much money. She was famous, and each engagement paid well, however these did not occur with sufficient frequency. Other conditions precluded her acceptance by either of the two concert monopolies in this country, so that the lucrative field of recital was closed to her.

But I also know a young man, blessed with a smooth lyric tenor voice. He has a good education; he is married and has four children. He is the head of the Voice Department in the Music School of one of our highly respected mid-west colleges. He has a splendid church position in a mid-west city. He receives many requests for appearances in the music of Bach and Handel. For the first time in several years he is on a short concert tour, but usually he is home for dinner every night with his family; he makes a comfortable income, owns a nice home, drives one of the better cars. He is not known in New York or Chicago. His teaching gives him an adequate living, and his singing engagements are the bonus in his profession. Is he a success? He thinks he is. He says, "This way, at least I can live, and live comfortably." He enjoys the truest kind of success. He is doing what he wants to do, and can live like a human being, besides. Examples like this could be multiplied on all levels.

When thinking of a career in singing as a "success," we must clearly define what we mean by success to the person involved. To one it means an all absorbing career, calling for forty weeks in the year on the road. It means the run of a theatrical production or the duration of an opera season, with its following concerts. To another person it means singing regularly in a large and important church, plus numerous oratorio and symphony orchestra engagements. On the other hand, there are those who prefer the field of entertainment and whose success is measured by the number of appearances on television and in radio, and the selling of a million copies of a single recording. Then there are a considerable number who prepare for a career in teaching, which, while not so remunerative from day to day, still assures a regular income adequate to maintain a family in a fixed place of residence. To this is added the prestige of fame as a private teacher or as the respected member of a university faculty. To a mother of growing children, success means a regular church position and occasional oratorio, concert and club engagements, which can be handled without much disturbance to family life.

No matter which branch of the Singing Art we prefer, the need for excellence in it is inescapable. This takes much study and preparation. While in the entertainment field the voice may be a secondary factor, there is nevertheless the need for much talent and hard work in the technique of "delivery." Here dependable rhythm, sense of pitch, diction, style, emotional freedom, and personality appeal are still challenging factors. There is also the limitation in such a field that is imposed by youth. Popular music is essentially the young person's field. True, there are a few hardy perennials still about, but usually their lasting power is in the field of dramatics, or personality, rather than voice, or the music they use. "Popular music must be music you can dance to," says one authority. Another says the emphasis is on intimacy. In any case, it is the music of youth, the teen-ager, with about twenty-five as the age limit of both performer and listener.

Singing is an exacting profession, but to those who make a careful study of what it takes, and who devote themselves to it with singleness of purpose, it is a very rewarding one.

The successful singing artist is the person whose desire to sing is sufficiently deep, strong and lasting to furnish the motive power behind all the work required and the courage to overcome all obstacles, delays and disappointments. When he decides to sing, he elects himself to distinction. When presenting himself to the public he expects the attention of all within range. He expects to be looked at and listened to. He expects people to put their thoughts and emotions at his disposal to be molded by what he brings. This demands a certain degree of natural talent, but granting that, much more is needed. A high level of proficiency is required in musicianship, vocal technique, diction, and in the capacity to study with meticulous detail. A highly retentive memory, and a clear mind are of course, also necessary. There must be good health, a reasonable degree of attractiveness, and an emotional capacity sufficient to move the feelings of others while keeping one's own under complete control.

Whether opportunity is found in the field of entertainment, show business, opera, concert, radio, television or in the church, the requirements are similar. The emphasis shifts a little in the different fields, but the ingredients are essentially the same.

Bing Crosby's book, *Call Me Lucky* has his picture on the cover. The intriguing thing is the pencil over his ear. A minor detail, perhaps intended to convey his easy going, nonchalant manner. But it means he is in business, a business which requires close attention to detail, and the pencil infers that in the course of preparation these details are noted, and not forgotten or overlooked. Rehearsals of popular songs for radio, or for a moving picture are as carefully planned and worked out as roles in grand opera or the finest of art songs.

The field of "popular" song music is thought by some to be the only way to make money as a singer.

But the test of a successful career is still, "How well does it last?" Every field, including that of popular song singing has its old stayers, but they can be counted on the fingers of one hand. The show business, and the field of light entertainment must be considered as something separate and apart from singing in the true sense of the term. Otherwise, we would have to admit that even Jimmy Durante is a singer. But he, voiceless as he is, would be the last to claim he was a singer. He is a comedian, an actor, and a good one, who has made a success of his profession.

Singing teachers all over the country recognize that since success in opera or concert in America is limited to a few gifted performers (most of whom are European), their pupils are quite likely to go to New York and try to find a place on

Broadway in a musical production or in radio or television.

Singing, and other forms of music, are now on a mass production basis. Through radio, television, records and the moving picture sound track, one singing artist is heard by thousands instead of a few. No longer does singing before a single local audience constitute success with a capital "S."

Even concert artists must go on long tours, appearing night after night before sizable audiences, over a considerable number of weeks. In this field people want "name artists." Concert subscription committees and symphony orchestras that engage them must be assured they are engaging artists of *proven* ability.

This does not mean there are fewer artists employed than formerly. There are many more in the public eye now than in the old days. But through mass production, public discrimination has also risen to a higher level.

The challenge to become an artist of proven worth is greater than ever, yet every season a number of new leaders come forward who have met it successfully.

CHARTING YOUR COURSE

In learning to sing, the first steps are usually the most important and need to be thoroughly agreed upon by teacher and student. It may not be necessary to determine the ultimate goal until the singer's potentialities have been uncovered. However, as the singer's association with the musical world continues, the various career possibilities may be recognized. Preparation for any kind of career must depend upon opportunity to prepare. A person is either so situated that he can plan for the necessary preparation or not.

The Student's Sources

The singer will recognize three basic methods of development which are open to him. There is, first of all, study with a reputable and dependable teacher. Second, observation of other singers. This formerly meant attending recitals, opera performances, and going to those places where artists could be heard who had reached the goals the singer sought. Today with recordings, and radio and television so easily accessible, it is a simple matter to hear the kind of singing the budding artist hopes to emulate, and to compare artists with each other as well as with himself.

A third method of development involves the singer's own thinking. This includes the development of his perception of values, his reasoning power, his capacity to judge his own experiences, and his devotion to practice and methods of study.

How To Select a Teacher

The selection of a teacher is a most difficult step for many. Some find themselves in an educational institution where choice is limited to members of that particular faculty, and then they are sometimes assigned rather than permitted to choose the instructor. When the student is free to select a private teacher, it usually is wise to choose one who has a good reputation for over-all success with those who work with him.

A reputation made because of the spectacular success of one or two "star" pupils is not a safe criterion. There may have been some exceptionally good ground work done somewhere else, or the "star" may be an exceptionally talented, thorough worker who lets nothing stand in the way, and who has a life philosophy that is bound to lead to success. Nor is the fact that the teacher was once a famous singer himself a safe criterion. Successful singers have thought in terms of themselves and their own voices for so long, they frequently find it difficult to think on the level of the student; but they sometimes become fine teachers after a few years of teaching experience.

The teacher who has learned to teach, who is a fine musician, a good linguist, and has a capacity

34

for inspiring leadership is usually best. Such a teacher shows a high level of progress with all students, is a strict disciplinarian, but a warm friend, and is loved and respected by all who study with him. The outstanding teacher is also up-to-date in repertoire, in good standing with the rest of the profession, ever alert to the professional interests of the young singer, and invariably emphasizes the fact that it is the *singer himself* who achieves the results.

Power of Application

To get to the top in the world of music, the student must endow himself with the power of application, that ability to hold oneself to a single focused objective and to travel in a straight line toward it. Some people take practice to mean mere repetition; that is not accurate. Practice must reflect *growth* and *improvement* while repetition of the task takes place. To repeat wrong habits over and over is wasteful and hardly improves the ability of the student.

Vocal and musical development will profit by the teacher's constant suggestions, based on what he hears when the student sings. Like a good physician he makes his diagnosis and prescribes remedies. Still, he knows that what he hears is likely to be imbedded deeply in the habit life.

If these memories and habits are defective, they can be replaced by newer accumulations of better habits which, through careful guidance, outweigh the old; and the conscious mind helps this change by a heightened awareness of the technique involved.

Every good teacher knows that he must frequently retrace with the student the path whereby the latter became conscious of a better way to sing a tone or interpret a phrase. Lasting progress is a rhythmic experience rather than a sudden burst of realization. It may seem sudden for a time, when the conscious mind first fully recognizes what is to be done. But the singer still has with him the old habits, ready to take over the moment he relaxes vigilance.

Practice Materials

Among the student's important practice materials are the devices and means whereby he either improves upon what he is doing or substitutes a new action for an old one. Certainly there are those who have been blessed with vocal talent and an instinct for clear vital sound. But there are many more who have achieved vocal power, range and beauty by patient *development* of the techniques of free functioning vocalization.

A student may have learned how to breathe, but may yet need to practice a great deal before he has developed sufficient breath control for a demanding phrase. Changes in vowel form change the resonance of the tone. Release from interferences induced by the effort to increase power or to sing high tessitura frees the tone, and therefore, increases its beauty, concentration and intensity.

These practices are all a part of tonal development. The muscles of the vocal instrument increase in strength through correct use. Thus, practice for reasons *beyond* the purpose of mere corrective procedure is not only justified, but is vitally necessary in a singer's career.

The body is never static. It is either growing and increasing its strength and efficiency, or it is becoming more limited and awkward. It is a physical law that the only way to increase the skill or strength of the body is to exercise it.

The great voices of Helen Traubel and Richard Crooks both demonstrate this principle. These fine artists had early opportunities to experience moderate success, for they were very gifted. However, they postponed entering "big time," and in comparative obscurity improved their voices. They worked for more secure control, depth, sonority, range and power of tone. They also labored diligently on repertoire, opera roles and recital material. When they had *practiced sufficiently,* they emerged, prepared to take their places as two of the finest artists this country has produced. While one may be born with the capacity for vocal greatness, the ability to use it waits upon development through patient well-directed work.

A PRACTICE OUTLINE

Now I propose to outline the program of a typical practice day. This of course is not put forward dogmatically; you will make what use of it you find appropriate.

I suggest that the first part of the practice period should be devoted to those light calisthenic exercises that result in "warming up the voice." These as a rule include some which have a *humming* effect, with the suggestion of release of the swallowing muscles or any others that might offer localized strength or reinforcement.

The first act then is to free the vocal tract so that the breathing system and the muscles used in articulation are released to perform their func-

37

tions. Conventional exercises with especial attention to pure vowels and accurate intonation should be used. These few minutes of limbering up the mechanism are well spent: we are so very prone to make the voice sound as we think it should, rather than let it sound as it does when released to function.

Second come those remedial or corrective exercises that have been suggested by the teacher. These truly test the intelligence. They try the soul, and prove the control a singer has over himself. Here he must dare to change old ways into new. He must concentrate on these as long as he feels he can do so constructively.

The next step calls for exercises in flexibility and agility. They are needed by all voices, from the highest coloratura to the lowest bass. Books for the purpose exist, and are usually included in the study of solfege, or a few characteristic exercises or appropriate song phrases can be memorized.

FLEXIBILITY AND AGILITY DEFINED

Flexibility in the vocal sense is the capacity to increase and diminish volume. It is the dynamic range of the voice. The *messa di voce* exercises, used either in phrase or in single tones, develop the range and the skill of dynamic movement. Nothing is more monotonous than a static voice of fixed volume. The singer's greatest enemy is monotony.

Agility exercises are demonstrations of accuracy plus speed. They include both the scale and staccato flights of the coloratura and the ability of the low bass to sing the couplets in a Schubert song, or the runs in the bass arias of the Messiah. They apply equally also to the work of the contralto, and of lyric and dramatic sopranos. One of the severest tests of agility lies in whether the singer can move from one pitch level to another without carrying with him the tonal adjustment proper to the preceding level.

The Important Element, Musicianship

Fourth, especially in the early stages of learning to sing, comes work in musicianship. Books of "technical exercises" are useful for this. They introduce in sequence the various musical devices a singer must be able to perform with proficiency. Among useful collections are those of Vaccai, Concone, Panofka, Sieber, Salvatore Marchesi, Mathilde Marchesi, and Bordogni; as well as compilations of Spicker and Marzo. Many teachers prefer to cover this ground by assigning songs which cover the same range of interval study, time, and rhythm patterns. This is entirely satisfactory *if they do it with graded consistency;* but they rarely do.

However, such teachers cannot be blamed for objecting to the intrusion into lesson time that such exercises represent; such practice may best be carried on separately, under the direction of a good coach-accompanist. We are speaking here of how a student organizes his study materials, which is not exactly the same as how he allocates his time. In any event, the work described above must be assiduously practiced if singers are to escape the charge, continually leveled at them by conductors, pianists, violinists and other instrumentalists, that they are notoriously poor musicians.

The teacher, after carefully evaluating the needs of the student, must decide whether graduated songs or exercises should be used to improve the musicianship of the latter. Further consideration of the preparation and interpretation of song literature will be found in Chapters 13 and 14.

Song Preparation

Let us now proceed to the study of that all important element upon which beautiful singing depends. If a song is used, its preparation goes through four distinct stages. First the song is learned. The best method of learning it depends on the stage of musical advancement of the student. Before anything else, set the tempo or the pace. For beginners it is sometimes wise to beat time with the hand while reciting the words in a spoken tone; the time value of notes, rests, retards and accelerations must be closely observed. Later the singer learns the musical pattern by applying his sight reading, or by hearing the song played on the piano. More advanced singers can learn the song at once, especially if they can play the piano.

Secondly the song must be memorized. The test of the memory comes at the moment recall is required.

The third stage of song preparation is the rehearsal or polishing stage. Here each phrase is re-examined for its accuracy, proper tonal quality and color, correct pronunciation and emphasis, and its contribution to the whole.

40

Fourth and last, the song is sung as a whole, and presented as a complete unit to those who listen. The song by this time should be "sung in" to the singer's consciousness so that it is indeed a part of him, like an inwoven thread in a piece of cloth. Thus by orderly systematic preparation the singer has made the song his own.

HOW A SINGER BREATHES

ALMOST EVERY WRITER ON SINGING HAS WRITTEN about breathing. Perhaps all that needs to be said about it has already been said. Certainly it has been the subject of much attention since the first trained singer appeared.

This is one subject upon which I urge my readers to keep an open mind, and listen to other opinions besides mine.

In different periods of vocal history, the emphasis has been moved from one element of the technique to another, until different schools of thought developed. To some it was purely a physiological experience. To others it was psychological and emotional, and you were urged to think away from it, guided by mental imagery. Others thought tone focus or quality controlled the breath, which placed control in the area of the word. Even the physiological approach needed to be clarified. Some breathed abdominally. "Belly breathing" it was called, and still is. Others emphasized the diaphragm and inter-costal rib

42

action. Others insisted that since the air filled the lungs, it was a chest experience.

One thing is certain. The breath is the source of tonal energy and correct breathing is the source of tonal beauty. The subject can be over-simplified until it is practically ignored, and it can be tortured by self-conscious effort until it becomes an obstacle to freedom.

Do we sing because we breathe, or do we breathe because we sing? This sounds a little like the old conundrum about the chicken and the egg; but it has tended to divide singers and teachers into two separate schools. I shall make the point that both sides are right, since there is a recipro-cal interaction between singing and breathing.

Balanced Pressure and Resistance

When we inhale before singing, speaking, or yelling, we act as automatically as when we draw back an arm to throw. Yet singing makes two special demands upon us: it calls for a breath supply in excess of normal and it also requires a new function: the act of balanced retention, which is another way of saying "resistance". By this double action the singer imparts vitality and in-tensity to the tone.

How much resistance depends upon the volume and intensity desired. It is like holding a book in your hand. The strength used is an automatic re-sponse depending upon the weight of the book. Add another book and the strength used is auto-matically increased. How much is determined by the demand.

The outward pulsation of breath is equalled by the adjusted vocal cords, the diaphragm and the resilient rib walls. The singer's subjective feeling is a sensation of buoyancy or vitalization rather than any condition that he himself could analyze in terms of physiology. In a good singer this sensation is not localized. "The whole man breathes," says Ffrangcon-Davies in *The Singing of the Future*. This is true: nature places subtle and mysterious forces at the singer's disposal. They are subtle but none the less real and tangible.

In everyday living, a person just inhales and exhales. But if he wishes to sing, he must breathe with added purpose. His tone must have the qualities of pitch, intensity, volume, duration and emotional color. There is a new need to be met, a new function to be learned. He must now retain the supply of air not yet used. When he has mastered the necessary balance between pressure and resistance he feels a state of exhilarated buoyancy, and his breath supply is available to the singing concept. At the point when he has become familiar with such an experience and has developed the strength to maintain it during phrases of average length or more, he has realized what is called *breath control. (See figure 1.)*

Inhalation

The inhalation of breath should never be noisy. It should never seem to resemble a gasp. Sometimes in the long phrases such as are encountered in the music of Bach or Handel, the singer uses a device known as "taking a breath on a breath." That is, with the unused breath still under control a singer adds a little, but this action should never be seen or heard.

Adequate breathing for singing is based upon physical, mental and emotional poise. There are people to whom inner tension, mental uncertainty

Figure I.

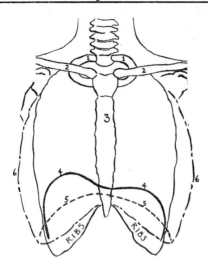

1. First Rib
2. Clavicle
3. Sternum

4. Diaphragm relaxed
5. Diaphragm depressed
6. Lateral expansion during inhalation

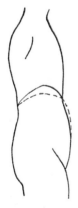

— — — — — Inspiration.

Abdominal wall relaxed.

Diaphragm contracted.

———————— Expiration.

Abdominal wall contracted.

Diaphragm relaxed.

45

and lack of concentration is a normal state of life. Until mental and emotional control are established, breath control will remain a problem.

POSTURE

The posture is the anchor of breath control. The singer who looks for automatic response from his breathing mechanism must check his posture with attention to these points.

1. He must stand on both feet, the weight slightly forward on the balls of the feet. It is even better if one foot is a little ahead of the other and most of the body weight is resting on the forward foot.

2. He must stand erect so that the weight of the torso, arms and head does not rest into the pelvic cavity. This calls for an erect spine, the surrounding muscles of which sustain this load. This is not an upward pull of the chest or shoulders, but rather an elastic stretch from below, upward. The strength necessary to retain this position may take time to develop. There should never be any abdominal sag.

3. The chest will then be high, i.e. medium high with the shoulders resting down, never lifted. One writer has suggested that the singer use as imagery the picture that marionette strings are attached to his sternum bone and the top of his head, and controlled from above.

4. The neck muscles should be relaxed so that the head can turn easily as on a swivel. Any slump in the position of the chest will pull at the muscles of the neck and throat. The elevated chest is, therefore, of prime importance. If we

straighten the spine, and (let me add) tuck the buttocks in and under, the following conditions exist: The abdomen is flat and firm, the intercostal region (lower ribs) is wide, the upper rib-cage is expanded to its capacity, the chest is high, and a sensation of equilibrium is realized.

To maintain this postural attitude while singing takes strength and training. When these suggestions are followed, it will be found that the skeletal muscles plus *the diaphragm* can furnish the strength needed to control pitch, tone quality, volume and duration.

As Westerman says in his book *The Emergent Voice,* "it is one of the minimal centers of control." Its function in inhaling is to draw air into the lungs. Its more important function is to furnish the resistance against the inward and upward pressure of the abdominal and intercostal muscles in the exhalation of breath while singing. It is never under direct control. It acts as a balancing force and tolerates no local sensation as a guide. Its real job is to deliver the breath to the vocal cords with whatever intensity or volume the mental image demands, from the most delicate pianissimo to the full strength of the voice. The diaphragm which is the body's most delicate and responsive nerve center is the instrument of expression.

Skills in Breathing

Most people breathe naturally, but few people breathe *adequately* for singing. These strengths and skills must be developed by practice and use. There is no substitute for skill. The guidance of a well-trained teacher, who understands both the mental attitudes and the physical conditions demanded by singing is usually required. Such skill sometimes develops through use alone, but not often. Even for the most talented, the time comes sooner or later when this function must be mastered as a technique.

Taking a breath should be a functional act. It should be an automatic response to achieve the result desired.

If the postural background is right, the lungs fill, and an expansion is felt within them. However, since the lower part of the rib-cage is more mobile than the upper, the movements which are the result of inhalation will be noted in the intercostal region.

We keep hearing much about the diaphragm in singing, but as mentioned earlier in this chapter, its action is spontaneous and therefore involuntary, unless the singer chooses to make it voluntary. It can be either or both.

When inhaling, and the elastic sponge-like mass of the lung cells expands, the enlargement will be felt as a slight widening of the rib-cage, and a descending of the diaphragm.

The singer is therefore more aware of the filling of the lower part of his lungs than the upper. That is why so much emphasis is laid upon deep breathing in singing.

Deep breathing should never be confused with "low breathing". The abdomen remains firm, but elastic. Consequently, both a lateral and a deepening expansion is noted. The downward movement of the diaphragm will not disturb the elastic firmness of the abdomen. Any *visible* bulging, outward or downward, is not necessary to good inhaling. The breath fills the lungs. The actual

48

displacement of both the diaphragm and that part of the abdomen just beneath is slight. In the best of singing artists it is rarely visible. The "feel" of expansion is mostly in the small of the back, and beneath the floating ribs, the intercostal region. The diaphragm and abdominal muscles will still do all they need to do.

As the singing act begins, a definite though slight contraction inward and upward will be felt in the abdominal area. Therefore the rhythm of the breathing function is downward-outward for inhaling, and inward-upward for exhaling. This is always functional and never a personally induced action. The shoulders and chest are never raised or lowered as a part of the breathing action.

While inhaling, it is important that all the muscles of the tongue, jaw, and mouth generally used in chewing and swallowing, be completely free of tension. They should be relaxed almost to the point of flaccidity. The diaphragm also should be left free, so that its action is functional. Under no circumstances should it be "used" to inhale. It should not bulge forward or outward. There may be a slight protrusion at the epigastrium, but this should result from inhaling.

Breathing and Mental Attitude

We have no direct control of muscles. We have no way of separating the breathing act from the emotional attitude it expresses. Muscles move because of mental imagery; therefore, it is a mistake to "work" the breathing system. We should let *it* work, instead.

However, if the tone is to be intense and concentrated, this action must be positive, firm and strong. As we begin to sing, the pressure of breath is resisted by the adjustment of the vocal cords. This retardation of breath results in compression of air in the lungs, which automatically brings into play the resistant strength of the chest walls and the diaphragm. When these forces of pressure and resistance meet, the result is an exhilarated buoyancy in the body, and a sense of strength in the larynx. The resistant strength seems to focus in the chest at the sternum bone. This was called the *appui* or *point de résistance* by Jean De Reszke, and the *appoggio* by the Italians.

Singing requires strength, energetic strength, but the energy is the "free wheeling" type, or similar to that noted in the hands of a virtuoso pianist, or in the limber swing of a bat by a good baseball player. It is a buoyant, vital feeling, firm but not rigid, free but not loose.

If the vocal cord adjustment is healthy and firm, there is clarity of tone and an economy in the use of breath that makes possible the singing of long phrases, and the nuances of vocal volume.

The Quick Breath

When a new breath is to be taken, the vital firmness of the vocal adjustment is momentarily released. The feeling is that of a very slight relaxation of jaw and a release of the diaphragm. When there is plenty of time to breathe, such coordinated action is no problem. But where quick breaths must be taken during long phrases or runs, then taking a "breath upon breath" may be practiced. In this case, the release is slight: all the breath has not yet been used, yet more breath will be needed to finish the phrase. Such momentary replenishment can easily be learned, but the release and adjustment of the vocal factors must be instant. Otherwise, the "quick breath" will be noisy.

An often repeated quotation of Lamperti's would apply here. "Never let anyone hear you breathe, never let anyone see you breathe, never let anyone observe that you are running out of breath."

All breathing work should be directed to the object of cultivating such breathing as a *habit*. The singing artist relies upon it as such, and therefore, is not conscious of its action as he sings. But if he neglects to establish an adequate breathing technique, he will find severe limitations imposed on his ability to sing.

EXERCISES FOR BREATHING

The following is a conditioning exercise for breathing. It should assist in developing efficient breathing as an almost automatic function.

Practice standing erect, keeping the body quietly balanced and poised, and the mind calm, and establish a buoyancy of attitude like that of the natural response to joy. Now inhale a full breath, with attention to the following points:

1. Inhale deeply with hands extended as in entreating. Let the lungs fill.
2. There will be a downward sensation as the diaphragm descends, causing an outward expansion of the lower ribs, back and front of the body, across the floating ribs.
3. Keep the throat free and relaxed, so that the breath will be ample and deep.
4. Do not consciously draw in air, but *allow* the breath to reach its ultimate point.

5. Stop when the point of satiation is reached. Do not force past the "point of comfort."

Now exhale the breath as follows:

1. Keep the body poised and alert.
2. Exhale gently (upward) through the lips as though blowing a trumpet, sustaining the expansion of the side ribs and the height of the chest as long as possible.
3. Retain the width and steadiness of the diaphragm with no sudden contraction or slump.
4. Allow no tension or slump in the upper part of the torso.
5. Exhale by releasing the muscles of the lower abdomen, toward the inward and upward action of these muscles. This contraction is slight at first, but increases until the abdomen is flattened inward.
6. Preserve the sensation that the upper part of the body is always equally fully expanded.

This whole experience, which is "natural" in the best sense, should be easy and pleasurable.

After repeating this exercise a few times, try one in waltz tempo. Take a short quick breath through the nostrils. Exhale in two sharp puffs with the lips compressed as above. This will make diaphragm and abdominal action evident, but the action should be so free that the exercise can be continued indefinitely without tension.

While silent breathing exercises may be of some benefit, they by no means result in the coordinated and balanced condition known as breath control. This can be found and strengthened only during the singing act itself. Varying pitches, vowels and volumes will make their demands upon the breath. Exercises and songs which require this balanced coordination are the only practical means of developing control.

THE TONE BEGINS

INTONATION, ATTACK, PRIMARY VIBRATION, THE beginning of tones, and the stroke of the glottis are all examples of the studio terminology intended to indicate the nature of the instant of phonation. Which one of these is the most acceptable depends upon the interpretation we give it.

Ideal circumstances, that is, body poised and alert, breath in a state of vitalized equilibrium with complete absence of tension lift or slump, will find the larynx at its own level of repose. The response to the intention to sing is one of the phenomena of nature. With perfect timing the breath impulse which automatically responds to the concept of pitch and word, is met by the definite approximation of the vocal cords. Thus the act of phonation begins. The vocal cords set the air impulse into vibration. Here we must guard against breathiness or that tightness which indicates that control is sought at that point.

The air stream is very slight. Good teachers and great singers have always advocated economy in the expenditure of air. Such approximation of the vocal cords depends on balanced control of breath. The successful approximation of the vocal bands cannot be realized if a singer tries to blow too much air through them.

As D. Ffrangcon Davies says in *The Singing of the Future*, "One should learn to emit just enough breath to make a whisper, and then convert it into tone." And W. J. Henderson adds, "This is what the old Italian masters meant when they continually told their pupils to learn how to 'filar il tuono' or 'spin' the tone." The air should flow out in a gossamer filament. When air is released before the attack an aspirate *h* sound is heard. When the vocal cords approximate first, the air must burst through; this makes a "clucking" sound. But when there is balanced coordination between a healthy throat condition and a free functioning breathing mechanism, a clear bell-like sound is realized. Prolonged, this instant of attack becomes tone, just as a point prolonged becomes a line. The stream of vibration thus set up by the generator is reinforced by the ventricles of the larynx, and by the laryngo-pharynx, oral pharynx, nasal pharynx, and mouth. Thus the primary vibrations become audible to the receptive ear as a vowel or humming sound. *See figure 2.*

The sensations of the participating elements, the pulse of breath, the adjustment of the vocal cords and the sympathetic adjustment of the resonators are below the level of consciousness. The effect is know only to the hearing. The only sensation worth mentioning is that of exhilarated freedom, plus a sense of firmness and health in the functioning parts. Any other sensation is

54

Fig. 2.

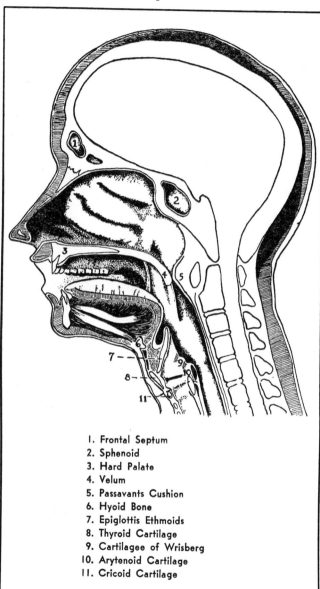

1. Frontal Septum
2. Sphenoid
3. Hard Palate
4. Velum
5. Passavants Cushion
6. Hyoid Bone
7. Epiglottis Ethmoids
8. Thyroid Cartilage
9. Cartilagee of Wrisberg
10. Arytenoid Cartilage
11. Cricoid Cartilage

Fig. 3.

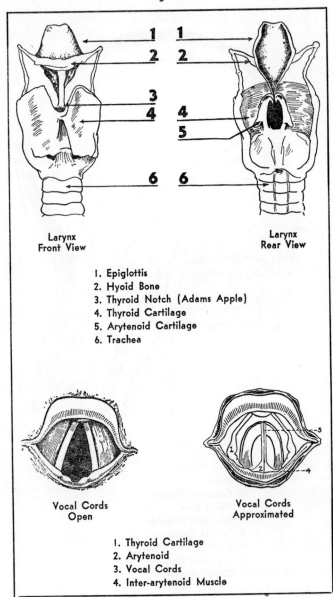

Larynx
Front View

Larynx
Rear View

1. Epiglottis
2. Hyoid Bone
3. Thyroid Notch (Adams Apple)
4. Thyroid Cartilage
5. Arytenoid Cartilage
6. Trachea

Vocal Cords
Open

Vocal Cords
Approximated

1. Thyroid Cartilage
2. Arytenoid
3. Vocal Cords
4. Inter-arytenoid Muscle

56

likely to be brought about by compensatory interference, nervous tension, or the effort to control consciously what should be a completely functional response.

When a sense of local control exists at the larynx, that organ is sometimes pulled out of position by muscles belonging to the swallowing action. These can be in the tongue or the sides of the neck, or at the point where the velum (soft palate) is drawn up and back, to prevent the entrance of air while swallowing and the escape of vibration while articulating voiceless consonants. While one is singing, all the muscles that ordinarily engage in the swallowing act must be left completely passive.

The entrance must be firm and accurate, and yet it must take place in an atmosphere of complete freedom. The firmness is not rigidity, nor is the freedom looseness. The vitalized breath imparts its vitality to the entire vocal mechanism. Those who think of it as a "stroke of the glottis" should compare it with stroking a cat. This is an act which picks up its contact while in motion, just as a violinist strokes the string with his bow.

RESONANCE

Resonance is that amplification and intensification of the fundamental element in the vocal tone which gives the voice character, richness, sonority and beauty. Since the fundamental quality of tone cannot be heard for any appreciable distance, resonance is really the substance of tone quality. Every vocal sound has its measure of resonance. Therefore, the character and quality of resonance is a matter of great interest to the singer. Resonance is a result, not a cause. One of the most common errors is the effort to produce resonance consciously, rather than recognizing it as the natural result of proper fundamental tone condition and impulses.

The two most prominent scientists who have interested themselves in this matter in recent years are Wilmer T. Bartholomew of the Acoustical Society of America and Dr. Kenneth N. Westerman. In this chapter I shall borrow from these authorities several quotations which have come either from conversations with them or from their printed works.

Dr. Westerman, for example, makes the statement that the study of resonance in the science of physics divides itself into two types of research. One is "the study of catacoustics or reflected sound and the other the study of diacoustics, or sound directly communicated to the ear from sonorous bodies." In any event, the size, shape, or the material from which the initial vibration, originating at the generator, is resonated must be able to vibrate in phase with the source, the generator, the vocal cords.

One of the reasons for discussing this subject here, is that neither the singing profession nor the physicists have been able to agree upon a terminology acceptable to both professions.

The clear thought of the pitch and word should find immediate response in both breathing mechanism and vocal cords. The breath flow is established by the inward and upward contraction of the abdominal muscles, an action so natural that in many singers it has never required any thought at all.

The "set" of the cords, the healthy natural action of the larynx, gives character to the fundamental tone quality. Here we encounter the first requisite to good resonance. Since resonance is the multiplication and enlargement of the original vibration, (actually their "re-sounding"), it follows that we are concerned with that which is enlarged and multiplied. This is the "attack," which must be clear, clean cut, and firm if good resonance is to be achieved. The response of the larynx is automatic or functional; therefore, control is found in terms of breath, vowel and pitch thought, rather than as a local muscular control. Once the "attack" is right, we may look for the conditions which determine the character of resonance. *See figure 3.*

The shape and size of the resonating areas are conditions that cannot very well be separated from each other. The vowel has great influence over the shape, size and level of these areas, and it follows that every singer should have vowel ideals which govern pronunciation while singing. He should so pronounce them as to give ample space in the throat, pharynx and mouth. *See figure 2.*

Here Mr. Wilmer T. Bartholomew steps in and reports that his findings show that the principal physical factor in tonal beauty or resonance is the large throat. He also calls attention to the fact that the muscles that open the throat are among the easiest to "surprise" into action.

In spite of many claims that resonance centers in the mouth, Westerman declares that vowel frequency bands vary enormously. We all know there are bright and dark vowels. The frequency of "oo" has been found at about 362 cycles per second, while the high rate of "ee" has been found at 3100 and 3200 cycles per second.

59

These vowel formants, (rates of vibration) influence, but do not control vocal resonance. For that we go back to Bartholomew's large throat in which the initial vibration, or fundamental, is strengthened.

We all know of the undesirable effect of a spread vowel; it loses line or intensity; a "breathy" vowel which loses its energy of impulse; or a "hooty" vowel which loses its impingement.

The vowel that maintains its "line" focus or impingement seems to be that which is based on humming regardless of whether the hum is used as a teaching device or not. Then there seems to be the openness of throat from the top to the bottom of the "tube," which agrees with the scientific findings of Bartholomew.

This does not mean that the vowel is drawn back in the throat. Its pronunciation is still forward and free, maintaining that vitality advocated by Louis Bachner in his book called *Dynamic Singing*.

Under such conditions there is always the sound of the nose in the tone, but never of the tone in the nose. It is important that such a differentiation be made, and the test by momentarily closing the nostrils with the finger tips is familiar to all.

The sustaining of the openness mentioned above is one of the primary considerations of the singer. Habits of pronunciation and vocalization will seek frequently to interfere with it, but the openness must be sustained, and the teacher must be prepared to hear and correct.

"Since resonance is an effect, a characteristic of sound, it follows that consciousness of it belongs to the realm of hearing rather than to sensation. One of the commonest errors made by singers is the effort to make the tone resonant and to feel it somewhere, rather than to allow it to be an effect produced by expressive motivations, plus a correctly functioning instrument.

"Thus in the act of singing there are two types of resonance involved and the reflector (the pharynx) must be of such size, shape and liveness or firmness that it can vibrate in phase with the source, the vocal cords."

If resonance is the result of vibration in space, it follows that we should treat tone as space, with its quality controlled by the ear, rather than by the sense of touch.

The fundamental causes of good resonance are then, a good clear attack, a pure vowel, a sustained tone level, and an ample sense of pharyngeal space. Singers frequently make the mistake of taking hold of the tone in order to control it, thereby robbing it of freedom.

Tone, however, is not a physical thing. It is the expression of a mental concept, and a feeling for expression. To result in good resonance, the mental concept must first be clear as to pitch and vowel, which should result in level and form. After that the resonance of a voice is affected in texture and color by the interpretive or emotional concept of the singer.

Emotion, or feeling, is recognized by every singer as a definite power resulting in very positive physical responses.

Summary on Resonance

Just now, let us briefly enumerate the requisites to good resonance and some of the errors to be avoided. The requisites are these:

1. Clear pitch through tone and concept
2. Clear vowel
3. An established tone level (hum)
4. A clean-cut attack
5. Sensitive dilation of the pharyngeal cavities
6. Effective breath control in terms of sustaining power
7. The "released" quality in tone

Among the common errors is the effort to localize resonance. Resonance is a "universal" not a localized thing, and it utilizes all the cavities of the head, throat and chest, and even the bony structure of the whole body. Any effort to localize the resonance would result in placing a limitation upon it, and would deprive it of that sense of detached freedom which is its life. A singer cannot safely "take hold" of his resonance; it must be released.

Of course all forms of interference must be eliminated. A stiff jaw, a depressed tongue, a tensed chin surface interfere not only with clear speech, but also with resonance.

Another common error is to imitate resonance by a thickening process in the mouth or nasal area which seems to enrich the tone quality, but which in reality muffles it considerably. Clear and released resonance will naturally seem to focus high and forward in the head, even though scientific tests do not establish this as a fact. We are speaking of sound as recognized by hearing, not by sensation. Since resonance is known only by its sound, and the singer himself listens to it only subjectively, he needs the discriminating ear of a teacher to guide its development.

ARTICULATION

Think for a moment about the miracle of speech. Thought and feeling require a medium of expression. The complex mechanism with which we are equipped for that purpose inspires a sense of awe and wonder. The speech mechanism is so sensitive, so alert, so responsive that it requires no local sensation of action to control it. The means by which control is acquired is rather a culture in sounds, a response to the effect of phonetic values upon the ear.

The first objective in singing is to convey meaning and its attendant feeling. A song is first a poem; an opera is first a play. The order of composition is first the idea, then the words, then the music they inspire. We should hold these elements in that order when we sing.

Too many people feel that the medium with which they sing is the voice. Edward Johnson, formerly one of the finest of our opera singers, and later manager of the Metropolitan Opera Company, once gave an unwitting illustration of the good artist's views on this matter. During a short address in Orchestra Hall in Chicago on the occasion when he was awarded an honorary doctorate, he spoke more or less as follows: "I have been in this hall many times, but always with my words and with my music. Tonight I find myself without words or music." An interesting thing here is that this leading operatic tenor, speaking of his own singing, never used the word "voice."

"Voice" . . . Should we think of this word as a verb or a noun? Is the "something" it refers to an act or a thing? Whatever its grammar, the voice acts only as a vehicle to convey the meaning found in language and music. They, the language and the music, are what is presented to the audience. My own teacher told me years ago, "Don't sing with your voice, sing with your expression." It is not easy to put the idea into words, but the student who grasps it has passed a critical milestone.

Most of the English speech we hear in our every day life is lamentably sub-standard. Flat, whining, harsh or guttural speech is often heard from otherwise cultured people. However, we do expect to hear pure English on the stage, in moving pictures, on the radio or in the pulpit; but even in these places we hear dialects, atrocious grammar, impossible usage, personal idiosyncrasies, unctuous elocution, or efforts to be "folksy" or stylistic.

When we hear pure English spoken or sung with clarity, with appropriate expression and without affectation, we recognize its beauty at once. We feel that one who speaks or sings beautifully wears a halo of distinction. Surely if we are ever to reach general recognition as singing artists, we must dedicate ourselves to the task of acquiring a skill and manner of delivery or words that will be both distinct and elegantly expressive.

Basic principles of good articulation in singing result in:

1. Easy understanding of the message
2. Presentation of a mood for the particular word being sung, the phrase, the song as a whole
3. Enunciation must leave the entire vocal tract free to perform its vocal functions.

The act of pronunciation is also the act of phonation. Vowel and tone are synonymous terms and are inseparable. The vowel form largely determines the conditions under which the sound is produced. Complete freedom of throat, tongue, jaw, lips and velum is necessary not only for elegance and distinction in speech, but also for beauty and control of tone.

Though many sing and speak the same language, no two people sound exactly alike, nor do any two have identical sound concepts. Backgrounds of culture, dialects, usage and other factors govern the speech of most people. Then, too, varying moods and degrees of emphasis govern the size and form of vowels and also the varieties of percussive intensity in consonants.

This variation in moods also governs the tone color of vowel sounds, but for our present purpose it is important to note that pronunciation changes with the changing desire for effect. This is evident in casual speech, where moods of joy or anger use pronunciation forms different from those of grief or tenderness.

DICTION

As a first principle, good diction must take place in a climate of freedom, where a free functioning vocal mechanism permits simple, clear and understandable speech, and where also linguistic facility has been developed. The movements involved in enunciation should leave the vocal organs without interference of any kind.

It is vitally important to be familiar with the tools of our trade, and to know how to use them skillfully. These are the breathing system, the larynx, the tongue, the hard and soft palate, the lips and the walls of the throat and nasal cavities. We usually think of them as organs of sound, but they are also the means by which sound is converted into language.

The Tools of Our Trade

Objectively the tools of our trade are vowels, consonants, pitch and the variations of pressure by which we achieve dynamic effect and color. The organs of speech, like the larynx, do not obey conscious direction. They lie below the level of physical awareness and are obedient only to mental imagery.

This does not mean that they cannot be made to act consciously. They can, but such action would be justified only as a corrective device.

Such distortions of functional activity as raising the tongue tip while sustaining a vowel sound, or humping the base of the tongue or pressing it back and down or tensing the lips or stiffening the jaw may need specific remedies to correct them. But such devices as may prove useful are temporary expedients and are not a part of normal vocal function.

It is of first importance therefore that we find proper "ear models" from which mental images can be formed, and here we meet our greatest difficulty.

We singers have two choices. We may rely upon pronunciation and vocal habits which result almost entirely from heredity and environmental influences, or we may decide, as consciously trained, self-determined individualized people, to establish our own linguistic models.

Voice is beautiful only when there is a beautifully effective word. Beauty of voice and beauty of word are synonymous terms; at least they are interdependent. Students of singing have concentrated to such a degree upon vocal tone that neglect of diction has become one of the glaring weaknesses in a singer's education. Good diction must be considered of *first* importance. The whole *raison d'etre* of singing is that it may effectively convey thought and feeling. The feeling may find some expression in tone color or dynamic nuance, but the *expression of thought* depends upon the intelligibility of words.

The first principle of artistic pronunciation is that it must be as simple, clear, and direct as possible. Its enemy is effort. Much of the faulty diction we hear is due to the fact that proper control has not been established. A singer whose tone control is not the result of balanced breath control will inevitably practice interference by over-energizing the speech parts. Another enemy of good diction is the habit of laziness or inertness in the tongue, lips, soft palate and oral pharynx.

The first thing to do is to release the tone from

67

all local effort, an objective gained through the right use of breath. Perhaps one of the most important factors to learn in achieving good diction is that pronunciation must not only be distinct, but the act must be released to the area of resonance, rather than held in the mouth as it is by so many singers and speakers.

Voice Placement

Vowels have form, level and direction. They are the only part of the singing act that can be said to have place. Indeed the term "voice placement" refers more to the position of the vowel than to the quality of tone. It is now obsolete because a tone is not a quality that can be put, held or confined anywhere. It is vibration in air. But in the experience of the singer a vowel is space that can have shape, size and a level of emission. One need only to sing a free humming sound to experience the channels for the emission of vibrating air. The space given to us for air lies in that area of the head above the lower edge of the top teeth. It includes the nasal pharynx (that part of the throat that lies above the larynx and behind the back teeth) the nasal passages and the mouth. All that lies below belongs to the swallowing function. The lower jaw is for chewing, the muscles below it extending down to include the neck belong to the reflex action of swallowing. The natural direction of this movement is back and down. The natural direction of singing is the upward and outward movement of air. Thus these two movements are incompatible and neither can be allowed to interfere with the other.

The tongue, lips and soft palate are constantly in action while pronouncing words, but their action is in the realm of effect instead of cause. While these parts must develop considerable dexterity and efficiency in enunciation, they do so only as the result of diligent practice of phonetic exercises with skillful agility in mind. This is an important point and is in direct contradiction with statements which call for trumpeting of the lips or conscious movements of the tongue and soft palate. A chart of phonetic sounds and how they are formed will be found in the next chapter.

When the singer is sustaining tones at a high pitch level, or producing sounds of considerable volume, radical enlargement of the vowel space may be necessary. Compared with casual speech this may appear a distortion. but dramatic utterance at high pitch levels is not casual speech.

Articulation Released to the Flow of Tone

When a singer has learned to use his voice correctly, (that is with freedom and with satisfying quality) he finds it necessary to conform all of his habits of vowel formation to the pitch level and tonal area he has established. This gives him the feeling of "releasing the vowel to the flow of tone," which, as has been said before, is the very keystone of good diction. He may even find that good singing diction *will oblige him to develop the use of an entirely new set of muscles.*

If a singer or a speaker by his pronunciation habits constantly interferes with free flow of tone, all the evil effects of interference result. Good vowel pronunciation, therefore, requires that the vowel be pronounced with an open throat, and released to the flow of tone rather than held in an arbitrarily fixed position.

What Is an Open Throat?

But let me warn you here of a common source of confusion. Remember when we talk of the throat we refer to that space which lies across the ears and behind the back teeth. An open throat does not mean a wide-open mouth. If you open the mouth widely in front, this actually has the effect of closing the throat. One teacher suggests opening the mouth to the width of the thumb, others talk of an opening two or three fingers wide. Opening the throat does not require that the front of the mouth be spread. When you open the throat it feels as though the ball-socket joint just in front of the ear releases the jaw so that it can drop slightly back and down, giving one the impression of the gentle beginning of a yawn. The full yawn tenses the throat, but the gentle opening just mentioned enlarges upward, backward and forward until a generous space is realized, which is quite different from the pushed down jaw and the widely spread mouth.

A common fault is the habit of pronouncing in such a manner that the vowel is formed in only a part of the resonance area, rather than having access to all of it. This is called "vowelizing the tone" instead of singing resonantly. The tendency of many singers to "sing forward" is largely responsible for this. Certainly vowels should sound forward, but they should also have height, depth and fullness. How are these effects to be obtained? By pronouncing the vowel in (or from) the area of the open throat, the nasal oral pharynx — that space behind the back teeth and across the ears— directly over the breath chamber, and on a line with the focus of the tone. Then if there is a com-

70

plete sense of release without collapse, the word will sound forward — outside.

Linguistic Facility

Consonants require another kind of treatment and study. Consonants are the framework — the bones of speech. They give the outline, the determining character of the word. In their articulation many physical parts are employed. The tongue at base and tip, the soft palate, the lips and teeth, all have their parts to play.

If we are to articulate our consonants effectively, we must be free of self-consciousness about them. The only remedy is again the clear thought of the effect desired, and the release of action to its performance. Consonants are either complete or partial interruptions to the flow of tone, but their action should be so rapid and spontaneous that tone seems to flow in a constant uninterrupted stream.

To accomplish the combination of flexible, sensitive, distinctness, and at the same time preserve tonal legato, should be the objective of every singing artist. This can be done by a clear conception of the effect desired plus that skill which comes only by continuous experimentation, observation and practice.

In the following chapter we shall deal with a detailed study of phonetic sounds. It should be sufficient to say here that such a study followed by thoughtful, careful practice is absolutely essential to an effective singing diction. Too many of our speech habits are instinctive, more the result of environmental influences than of applied standards.

71

Eloquent Enunciation

Artistic diction implies more than speech that is easily understood and elegantly delivered; it means that the emotions shall find expression as well. A vigorous and fervent utterance will have a different effect from one which is delicate and infused with a beautiful finesse. At times, of course, the artist will attempt to achieve finesse. Each has its proper place according to the situation.

The varying grades of intensity required by artistic singing place a further demand upon articulative agility without which singing loses much of its beauty and effectiveness. Here again, only skill, the result of intelligent analysis, observation and faithful practice will bring the necessary results. Let us remember there can be no really artistic diction without idealizing vowels above their ordinary value in casual speech. The same is true in the use of consonants. Special attention should be given to vocal consonants such as 'm' 'n' 'l' and 'ng', for to be heard distinctly the tone must freely "hum through" with the same freedom and level that it does in vowel sounds.

When diction becomes the product of the singer's mental models, it will bear individual characteristics.

Everyone who sings knows how to hum. He has hummed since he was a baby. The vowel line is a hum with a thought having taken form. As the forms change, they should do so with much ease and freedom; they should seem to dissolve into another.

Indeed the subject of vowel sounds and their control must be approached empirically if the vowels are to be pure. Let the scientists have their arguments about fixed or adjustable resonators, tongue or mouth positions, and whether or not the velum moves forward away from the "cushion of Passavant." These men give the singer nothing. Even when they point out that the line of tonal focus is nasal, it means nothing. All that is important is that the sound must be free; it cannot be confined. Tensions which hold a tone in place are always wrong, but if a singer's throat, palate and tongue are released, he knows only that he feels free to sing.

PHONETICS

THE ACTS OF PRONUNCIATION AND OF PHONA-
tion occur as one. Beauty of voice and beauty of
speech are interdependent. The best way for a
singer to improve his singing diction is to improve
his speech. This can be done in many ways, and
some books which present exercises in linguistic
facility will be mentioned at the end of this
chapter. Another way is to alert the mind to
linguistic values so that differences in speech
sounds are quickly perceived and evaluated. This
implies an ear training similar to that of the
musician, and indeed quite as important.

While speech teachers keep insisting that the
dialect of a certain region is the norm for the
people of that region, yet we of the singing world
insist that a standard of beautiful American
English may be established, colloquialisms and
dialects notwithstanding. Even though schools of
dramatic art teach their students to say 'neh-oh'
for 'no', an alert musician would quickly recognize
such an affectation. Anyone with even half an ear

can distinguish an 'aw' from an 'ah'. So we might go through the entire language and learn its purest, clearest, unadulterated sounds. The Germans and the French have definite standards, and yet those countries abound in dialects.

There is a Standard

This writer insists there is a standard of clear, unadulterated, distinguished American English. He has heard it spoken and sung by Americans. The late Reinald Werrenrath was an excellent example, and anyone who heard him perform *The New Life* by Wolf-Ferrari will agree that he used beautiful English in both the singing and speaking parts of that fine baritone role.

The principal difficulty in setting up a standard is the anomalous connection between English spelling and pronunciation. The singer or speaker deals in sounds, not orthographic signs. While there are only twenty six letters in the English alphabet, and four of them are duplications of other sounds, there are altogether between forty and fifty distinguishable sounds; this is not counting those essentially foreign. For each of these sounds there is a phonetic symbol. Through the International Phonetic Association a symbol has been established for each of the speech sounds of all standard languages.

These sounds are the vowels and consonants. Vowels are the space chamber, the vibrating and resonant area, the body or "meat" of vocal sound. The consonants are the complete or partial stops in the flow of sound, that give outline, framework and percussive value to words.

The table of I. P. A. symbols for the sounds of English speech appears below:

(i)	beet	(u)	boot	(ʃ)	sure
(ɪ)	bit	(h)	hay	(g)	goal
(e)	pay	(b)	bay	(k)	coal
(ɛ)	pet	(p)	pay	(m)	sum
(æ)	pat	(v)	vine	(n)	sun
(a)	ask	(f)	fine	(ŋ)	sung
(ɑ)	calm	(ð)	thy	(l)	led
(ɒ)	hot	(θ)	thigh	(ɹ)	three
(ɔ)	bawl	(d)	dye	(r)	red
(ə)	the	(t)	tie	(w)	witch
(ʌ)	cut	(s)	seal	(hw)	which
(o)	tone	(z)	zeal	(j)	you
(ʊ)	foot	(ʒ)	azure	(ç)	hue

With the inclusion of the following symbols, most of the sounds of French and German are included.

(y)	French u	(ø)	French eu and German ö
(Y)	German ü	(x)	ach

The special diction problem for singers is that sounds in singing are often prolonged far beyond their usual length in speech. To this variation in length of sounds is added the changes of pitch and volume or stress. While the singer maintains a steady and continuous tone, he must introduce the necessary variations in sounds. If there is adequate breath control and complete freedom of all the speech parts and in the vocal tract, the voice will be free to function in terms of all three of these variants. When the singer must modify vowel sounds or pitch levels, he must do so with ease and freedom. This should be done so efficiently that the listener is unaware of the change.

Both teachers and singers are strongly urged to study and learn the International Phonetic Alphabet to the degree that they can not only recognize and pronounce the symbols and read any passage of English that is written in the phonetic alphabet, but also so that they can transpose any passage or word into phonetic script. Perhaps one cannot expect complete perfection in the completion of this task immediately, but it should be practiced.

Exercises to improve the efficiency of lip action, to awaken lazy tongues and to release the uvula and palate will be found necessary in this day of sub-standard American speech. A teacher should be able to write the phonetic symbols over every word that is poorly pronounced, and to indicate what syllables and consonant forms should be stressed and which should not.

The following references are just a few of the excellent texts which are available to the interested student who wishes to improve his verbal ability.

1. Kenneth Thomas, *Introduction to the Foundation of American English,* Ronald Press.
2. Hugh R. Walpole, *Foundations of English for Foreign Students,* University of Chicago Press.
3. Gertrude Walsh, *Sing Your Way to Better Speech,* E. P. Dutton & Co.
4. Madeleine Marshall, *The Singer's Manual of English Diction,* G. Schirmer, Inc.

REGISTERS

THERE IS A SUBTLE, GRADUAL, BUT DEFINITE change in the quality of the vocal tone as it moves from one pitch level to another in singing. This variation of timbre is common to all musical instruments, but is particularly noticeable in voice because it is self-produced.

Some people claim there is no such thing in a singer's experience as registers, that they are illusions, and that in an evenly produced voice, registers do not exist. Others seem to be equally emphatic in declaring that there are three registers: chest, medium, and head, and can point to chapter and verse in many a noteworthy book on voice to authenticate such a stand. Some of these quotations go back as far as the early seventeenth century when the cultivation of the singing voice had hardly begun. Since that time the school called *bel canto* came forward with the theory that there were but two registers: one called *voce di piena* or full voice, the other *voce di finta* or the fine or spun out voice.

Many singers have serious register breaks or obvious changes in tone quality at certain pitch levels; others can sing from extremely low notes to extremely high ones without such breaks or changes; so it appears that there must be some simple explanation for a physical fact, which after all, must obey some physical law.

There is such an explanation. The voice is a functional instrument and gives no trouble as long as it is allowed to function freely. Only when conscious effort interferes with natural function will a singer feel a physical sensation of register change.

The Acoustical Change

Acoustically, nevertheless, a person with a good ear hears a change in the tonal texture. He will hear it in brass instruments, too. He will note that the piano, consistent in scale though it may be, has a marked difference in quality in different octaves.

Let me present an analogy to make my point clearer. Picture a glass of rich milk. It is opaque and somewhat creamy in texture. Gradually dilute the milk with water and at the same time permit as much liquid to run off as is added. Continue that process until finally the content of container is crystal clear water, letting light through and seemingly transparent.

One who is vocally free will experience a similar change in the ascending scale, from the thicker heavier sound to the lighter and more transparent; but as sound, and not as sensation. It will seem to thin out, and to give the impression of lightness and thinness. The quantity of liquid in the glass remains the same in volume, just as the

79

light thin air on the mountain top fills as much space as the heavier air below. Its substance, however, seems to have changed in texture. So also the substance of tone "melts through," proving the throat adjustment to be dynamic or pliable instead of static or fixed.

Vocal freedom is experienced when the voice moves from one pitch level to another with practically no sensation of change. Physiologically there are frequent changes of breath pressure, vowel form and tonal intensity, but these are responses to pitch changes rather than causes.

The Heavy and the Light Mechanism

The lower third of the vocal range is called the heavy mechanism by some and the chest register by others. This is because the vibrations seem to find their major reinforcement in the chest area. As the pitch rises, the vocal cords are dampened or closed at their extreme ends, until in the highest part of the vocal range only one third of the vocal cord length appears to vibrate.

Between the heavy and the light mechanism lies the middle part of the voice called by the French the "mixed voice." This has the character of both the light and the heavy in gradually changing degrees. Thus we could easily agree with those who claim the voice has two registers and those who claim there are three, since the "middle voice" is neither heavy nor light, but a varying mixture of both.

The "Lift"

Singers and teachers need a terminology to describe what they experience while singing. As a result, certain terms have come into use and deserve clarification. Witherspoon spoke of the "lift" in the voice, and others use the same term to describe the transition from the lower to the upper part of the vocal range.

There is a point in every voice where the texture of tone perceptibly lightens. At this point some singers may sense an added buoyancy of breath and others may not. But many teachers are keenly aware of the transition and seek to guide the student through a series of semi-tones which might otherwise be weak or threaten to "break". In any event the student should avoid "pushing up the chest," or carrying the heavy adjustment too far up the scale.

"Covering"

"Covering" and "vowel modification" are terms also frequently used to describe the functional changes in tongue and pharyngeal positions when ascending into higher tones. It is important that we understand that these changes take place in a free tonal emission so that we do not instinctively resist them. It is equally important that the singer does not give evidence that these are conscious or mechanical maneuvers on his part.

The even voice results when balanced breath is in control, and the entire musculature of tongue, jaw, and jaw hinge move freely and independently. Their movements are then concerned only with articulation and not with positioning the larynx and throat. These are left to function. However, freedom must not be confused with looseness. The throat structure should be firm (vital) but never rigid; free but never loose.

The changes in tone quality are brought about

81

by the fact that nature must produce a considerable range of pitch and intensity, by means of a pair of vocal bands about as long as one's little finger nail. These changes can take place only while the singer is content to let the voice function freely, rather than to attempt to make it sound in accordance with some preconception as to how it should sound.

THE CONCEPT OF TONE

We are constantly reminded that singers sing in accordance with a mental concept of tone. But it is not always made clear how that concept is determined. Certainly imitation of other voices, however beautiful, is not a safe guide. The only way to arrive at one's tonal ideal is to completely *release* the voice and let the desire for an expressive effect (rather than the image of physical tone quality) be the guide.

Someone once said, "The most beautiful tone possible to you is that sound which is your own native natural expression, rather than some sound produced in accordance with a 'method'." When the voice is relieved of the compulsion of the singer's mental expectancy as to quality, the voice becomes *itself*. In that state of freedom, register breaks, weak spots in the scale, and limitation in range are unknown.

Tests of Freedom

There are several sure ways of testing whether or not this ideal state of vocal freedom has been attained. One is adequacy of vocal range. The entire compass of the type of voice possessed by the singer, will be available when the voice is free. Therefore, range is a by-product of function rather than an end in itself.

So also with power: Vocal strength is the result of the development which follows naturally; it is composed of such elements of pressure and resistance as are involved in producing concentration and intensity in the tone quality, when the voice functions freely and, as a result, the singer's feeling is given free play. Again, in vocal power we have a by-product of freedom of function plus development. It must be understood that the vitalized control of the center of vocal energy, the breath, is constantly implied in these observations.

The remaining test of the free functioning voice is its flexibility. Can the singer diminish and cresendo in vocal power and intensity in all parts of the range? Of the two, diminishing will require the greater degree of strength and control. We rarely find the capacity to diminish to a point of vanishing pianissimo without losing the carrying vitality of the tone. Of course singing softly never means singing weakly.

In the final analysis, one could agree with either the proponents of the two-register or the three-register schools. A free voice will have a definite "chest" or heavy sound in the lowest part of its scale. It will also have a definitely fine, light, or "heady" sound in the upper third of its range. In the octave in-between there will seem to be an involuntary adjustment to the pitch level of each note, leading some authorities to say,"There is a new register on each note." However, that may be, with the vitalized breath furnishing the

83

strength with which one sings, free from interference in the vocal tract, and in a mind which anticipates pitch mentally, there can always be effective intonation on any pitch within the voice range. There must never be any slurring or sliding from one pitch level to another, lest the adjustment proper to the previous pitch be carried into the next one. The teacher's ear should always be alert to correct the fault. This lack of clarity in musical thinking has brought about much of the difficulty laid at the door of register changes. There are none in the properly used voice.

VOICE CLASSIFICATION

A mistake in the classification of a voice is a serious one. Yet, it is often made, and is all the more serious because it is most frequently made by those who teach or lead young singers. Choir and Glee Club Directors in a sincere effort to obtain a balance of choral parts will have a high baritone sing tenor or bass. Sometimes they will ask a lyric soprano, who is a good musician, to sing with the first altos.

The general division of voices is soprano, mezzo soprano, contralto, tenor, baritone and bass. There are several subdivisions of each of these classifications, which are of importance because they determine the musical literature used by that voice, and therefore, have a direct effect upon singing habits.

The subdivisions of the soprano voice are: the lyric coloratura, the lyric, and the dramatic soprano. Even the lyric soprano has quite recognizable subdivisions as for example, the lyric who would sing *Manon* by Massenet, would be a quite different voice from the lyric who would sing Butterfly in *Madame Butterfly* or Mimi in *La Boheme*. So also, the dramatic who would sing *La Tosca* or *Cavalleria Rusticana* would not be the ideal choice for *Die Walkure, La Gioconda* or *Aida*.

Among mezzo sopranos there are those who are almost sopranos and those who are almost contraltos. The same tendencies are noted in baritones. Some are almost tenors and some, almost basses.

Each type of voice has its degree of qualification for designation. This difference in degree is found in the texture of the tone quality, and not in the vocal range. This is why many individuals are deceived. They think the pitch range or compass determines the classification. The fallacy of this concept is found in the fact that many lyrics can sing lower than some mezzos, and many mezzos can sing higher than some lyrics. This overlapping or compass is found in every classification.

The determining factor is the tonal texture. The judge is the ear of the listener. Physiologically, however, the difference is in the glandular structure and balance in the body. Dr. Paul J. Moses of Stanford University says that voice classification can be recognized in body structure and skin texture, and that these contrasts should be quickly noted by the competent voice teacher. He places emphasis on the fact that every singer's voice possesses a measure of both male and female qualities.

The most feminine type of woman's voice is the lyric-coloratura. As the tone-quality gradually deepens more and more "maleness" appears. Thus the dramatic soprano and contralto usually have a larger and heavier body structure than do their higher-voiced colleagues. The same can be said for men's voices. The high light thin voices suggest a greater degree of feminine qualities than the bass or the baritone. Oddly enough these vocal characteristics do not necessarily extend to the mental life of the individual. Hence, the lyric tenor may be thoroughly masculine as a personality, and even more so than some basses. We are speaking of voices, not of personalities. The differences dealt with here are physiological and not necessarily personality traits. As an illustration, suppose we imagine clear water in a test tube. The clear water represents the "head tone" or falsetto sound in the voice. Now as we gradually mix particles of clay, the liquid grows thicker. Soon we have the light lyric, then the "dark" lyric, then the dramatic, then the mezzo and finally, when the contents of the tube are about evenly divided and well mixed, we have the contralto voice. The same imagery could be applied to the male voices.

Changes in Voice Levels

Voice textures can change. As singers develop in feeling and experience, and grow more mature, influences formerly hidden come to the surface. If freedom from repression or inhibition is experienced, the voice may go higher. This sometimes takes place after an artist has "arrived" in Grand Opera, but most frequently it occurs between the senior year in high school and the age of full maturity at thirty or thirty-five. When these changes are taking place, they must not be

86

held back. Singers frequently have commitments in churches, radio programs, or in some other kinds of professional work, and they fear to change lest they lose their positions. Sometimes, voice teachers are too quick to place a label on a singer, and then are afraid to admit they were wrong if the voice goes up or down.

Voice classification in a free functioning voice will reveal itself, but it sometimes takes a long time if the personal development of a singer is involved. There are plenty of singers with good voices who have never known what true freedom in *feeling* really is.

A singer with his vocal mechanism functioning at a true point of repose, whose feeling is released, and capable of exhilarated vital expression, is sure to be properly classified when comfort and peace of mind and body are the criteria.

FLEXIBILITY AND AGILITY

THE SINGER WILL WANT BOTH FLEXIBILITY AND agility in his singing, for they are both very necessary to artistic performance.

Flexibility belongs to that elastic, plastic kind of voice which enables one to move from one volume of tone to another with fluent ease. The manner in which this movement takes place can give as much meaning to the listener as the content of the words and music. It is obvious that a tone that is capable of expressing every conceivable emotion or mood must be a completely free tone. Such a tone is one based upon the free function of the voice in response to feeling, rather than a fixed quality produced for its own sake. A voice which is allowed to function freely is controlled by breath and vowel concept rather than by fixed extrinsic muscular strength.

Flexibility can be said to have range such as pitch has. A singer's dynamic range will go from his softest pianissimo to his fortissimo; this range grows in proportion to his vocal development. A flexible voice also colors automatically with every changing mood of the singer. It is readily responsive to feeling and is the vocal means of giving audible expression to creative imagination.

Flexibility of tone also allows vocal as well as verbal accent, by which important words and syllables are stressed. It underlies all feats of vocal agility. It is an indispensable element of the technique of an interpretative artist. But how is it acquired?

Developing A Flexible Tone

A flexible tone is elastic—it gives the impression of flowing easily, of being released without losing the basic vitality of quality. It is established by the condition that Louis Bachner calls the "hook-up," known acoustically as the "fundamental." This is the release of vitalized breath, resisted by the adjustment of the vocal cords in the larynx which in turn are aided in that resistance by correct posture.

All education and training are accomplished by means of differentiation. In the case of flexibility, it is becoming aware of that area in which a singer is as strong as a dancer or skater is in keeping his balance. Agility needs that release which makes grace and speed of motion possible. The strength is in the posture and the vitalized buoyancy of the body. The release is in the articulation and in the flow of warm breath.

This places the responsibility for control entirely upon balanced breath where it belongs, while the singer releases the word to the "flow of tone." If he keeps a conscious control upon the tone or the word, flexibility becomes impossible.

There is still some difference of opinion over the choice of devices to be used in the cultivation of flexibility. One suggestion is to sing short scales in easy range. Emphasis should be placed on the purity of the vowel sound while maintaining a vowel line through the use of the hum—not as a sustained sound to develop resonance, but merely to illustrate a sense of level and direction for the flow of sound. Once this seems secure, more sustained tone may be used, always avoiding any strain in an effort to develop range or volume. This can be done by practicing portamento intervals with a slight suggestion of crescendo in ascending. Later the famous *messa di voce* exercise of the early Italian teachers may be used. This begins with a single tone on a single vowel with the softest pianissimo possible, gradually increasing the power until full forte is reached, then a slow controlled diminuendo to return to the point where the pianissimo began. When properly done, this is a strenuous exercise and fatigue should be carefully avoided.

The same idea executed on the five or nine tone scale is also effective in developing the breath control upon which flexibility depends. The ability to diminish the last word in a phrase to a vanishing point, without having to end the word abruptly is a feat of technical skill which is an important item in any singer's interpretative repertoire.

Agility in Singing

Agility is rapidity and facility of musical execution. It demands lightness of touch in the approximation of the vocal cords, accentuated rhythms, and a completely free functioning vocal mechanism.

Agility is demonstrated in various ways. First, by a perfect legato—that smoothness of tonal transition from pitch to pitch and word to word without change or disturbance in the vocal adjustment, nor momentary interruption in the flow of sound. This accuracy and clarity must extend to the rapid execution of scales, arpeggi, appogiatura, acciacatura and other forms of musical notation. Clear staccati are an evidence of vocal agility. In addition to being an excellent exercise for the development of strength in the automatic vocal adjustment, staccati also encourage clear pitch thinking, pure vowel enunciation and breath control. Absolute pitch control cannot be taken for granted. However good a musician the singer may be, it still takes an agile voice to sing accurate pitch in rapid passages, particularly those which require scales, rapidly repeated notes, couplets and any other kind of rapid musical movement. The music of Mozart, Schubert and Bach presents many such tests. While the ballad or popular song singer may not be as interested in this technique as the singer of serious music, yet scooping, flatting and sharping has ruined many a career in the field of public entertainment. Pure intonation requires an agile voice. Fast scales are necessary to vocal elasticity. They should never be omitted from daily practice. They become the calisthenics of voice.

Speed and accuracy cannot be developed by practicing slowly. The demand for accuracy of intonation plus agility of movement must come from the auditory centers of the mind. In other

91

words, this skill is based upon an alert attitude plus a nimble musicianship.

Many times inaccuracy or inadequacy in florid passages is due to sluggish pitch *thinking* rather than clumsiness of voice.

The techniques of flexibility and agility often become confused because of the tendency of so many people to use the terms interchangeably. Flexibility is freedom of movement in terms of dynamic contrasts and tone coloring, while agility means feats of musicianship which are possible only after long hours of drill have established adequate breath control.

Use of the Trill

We have spoken about some items of vocal ornamentation but the final test of agility is the trill. A trill is the rapid execution of two notes of approximate pitch, under the same conditions that govern the singing of a scale; in fact a trill is a two note scale rapidly sung.

One exercise to develop the trill follows: Practice singing two notes a major second apart in the upper third of the vocal range, starting with the upper note. Sing them in steady tempo, *accenting* the upper note and treating it as a short grace note.

Then repeat, accenting the *lower* note, but accenting it as if it were a grace note. After singing these exercises for a time, suddenly double the speed.

Then sing them as notes of even value but in three speeds, the first rather deliberate and the others much faster. Think of them first as quarter notes, then eighths, sixteenths and thirty-seconds. After a while the larynx becomes accustomed to this oscillation automatically, and the trill appears. Should the major second be reduced while trilling to a minor second or less, practice the above exercises on a major third instead of a major second.

There are many singers who never need to go through this detailed process in order to trill. They sometimes do it imitatively after hearing it in another voice, and sometimes find more success starting right out into a rapid trill instead of building up the speed gradually as does the instrumentalist. This kind of trill however, is more likely to be the old Italian idea of a "shake" than a complete musical figure.

The development of a trill should be required of all singers. Baritones, basses and tenors need this proof of vocal agility as much as any other type of voice. Both flexibility and agility are the result of patient and continuous practice and experience. This is the price all must pay for vocal skill.

INTERFERENCES AND THEIR CORRECTION

MOST SINGERS HAVE HAD THE EXPERIENCE AT ONE time or another of confusing cause and effect. They have felt that muscular movement was cause and the tone the effect. Exactly the reverse is true. The anticipation of effect is cause; and the body responds—if it can.

Effective singing can be realized only when the vocal instrument is free to function normally. This function occurs in response to certain stimuli which have their source in the auditory centers of the brain.

The mental image of the desired result directs the musculature of the vocal instrument much as the eye muscles adjust the sight to different distances. But before such action can be free, the singer must respond repeatedly to these mental images. His response, moreover, must take place with the body in correct position, and the activity of the vocal instrument sufficiently released and *strengthened through practice* to meet the auditory demand.

Because so many people try to sing before these necessary background conditions are established, compensatory and sometimes unsatisfactory actions take place in the instinctive effort to produce the desired result.

Listing the most frequently found vocal interferences would practically amount to stating the experience of most singers in learning to sing. Usually an interference is the carrying over into the singing act of some undesirable habit of vocal expression acquired early in life. Language as it is spoken, at home or in the community while a child is growing up, always has certain patterns of muscular activity associated with it. Sometimes these habits favor singing and sometimes they do not. The Italians are instinctive singers because the liquid euphony of their spoken language lends itself to the freedom required by the singing act.

Dialects and Substandard Speech

Dialects and habits of substandard speech are often the primary causes of vocal interference. If vocal interferences are to be eliminated, the speech habits of the singer should be the first to come under scrutiny.

Imitation

Hearing other singers often results in an unconscious effort to imitate another's tonal quality. (Never teach by imitation). Since the other person produced the effect with an entirely different set of feeling impulses, and a different physical equipment, imitation of the quality of sound heard requires a conscious effort. This substitute for the singer's own natural expression is therefore

95

artificial, and interferes with the normal vocal function.

Teachers and singers do not always know that the sound they hear is not necessarily the true sound of that voice, but the *impression* which that sound has made upon them. That impression is frequently influenced by their own experience and association with other voices, as well as by their own voices. Good hearing is awareness of the inherent natural expression of the person heard.

Pronunciation

The pronunciation of a vowel and the act of phonation (producing the sound) occur as one act. Pronunciation induces the phonating energy, gives the *sound* of the voice form, shape or outline and establishes the conditions necessary for its continuation. A vowel concept finds response in the position of the vocal cords in the larynx, in the position and action of the tongue, the condition of the jaw, and in the action of the lips and of the soft palate. Only a mental image of the result desired could determine the nature of such a complex action. Consequently the vowel model must be established with as much care and with as much effect upon the tonal result as the concept of pitch. It is of primary concern to the singer and the teacher.

When vowels are not pure, clean, free and simple, tonal distortion follows, and with it of course, comes vocal interference. The faulty condition is corrected by conforming the vowel pronunciation to the highest ideal of the language, and by completely *releasing* the vocal instrument toward its realization, regardless of any disagreement with past habits.

Setting the Voice

Another source of interference is the tendency of many singers to "set" the voice. Instead of letting the voice function freely, they lock it into a fixed quality. Some have the habit of trying to control breath at the throat. Freer functioning would give the voice whatever tone quality is appropriate to the feeling expressed. Tone is not *produced* as such. It is a functional response *to an act of expression.* When it is so released it is not fixed and static, but dynamic and fluid.

Preventing Transition

This leads us to another source of interference and that is the habit of carrying the color, texture or quality of the tone from one register into another. (See Registers) This applies to all voice classifications. High voices tend to continue the vocal adjustment of the upper part of the range down too far, with the result that low tones are weak and ineffective. Most low voices have the constant temptation to carry the weight, richness and fullness of their lower tones into the ascending scale. When they do, a pushing effort and shouting often result.

The extreme method of starting the high notes in a very high falsetto, and contrasting that with heavy coarse low notes, and calling these adjustments the light and heavy mechanism has not been found uniformly successful, although it does have its passionate disciples.

Register Problems

Register interference is encountered in relatively few singers. When these interferences occur, they cause serious self-consciousness and vocal limitations. Those who suffer from this need the guidance of a reputable teacher who possesses a sensitive ear, a clear understanding of the phenomenon, and a reassuring manner of dealing with it. Every singer must learn how his vocal mechanism adjusts for changing pitch levels, and also how articulation varies for changing pitch levels.

Clumsiness or Awkwardness

Interferences often result from clumsiness, awkwardness, or lack of mobile facility in the articulation of words. Consonants are called "the bones of speech." But in singing their action must be so swift, so facile that the words are not only easily understood, but they also must leave the vocal tract so free that the flow of legato tone proceeds without perceptible interruption except where especially declamatory effects are desired. This calls for increased facility in articulation which many people cannot realize except by patient practice and faithful application. Consonants divide into such classifications as voiceless, voiced, fricatives and sibilants, and vary in percussive intensity. (There are further subdivisions of these classifications.) Few people arrive at a state of excellence in singing without skillful agility in the articulation of consonants.

Vocal interferences assume different forms. Those most frequently encountered are: thickening and stiffening of the tongue muscle, or any part of the swallowing, sucking, chewing group, resulting in tension in the larynx, rigidity or over activity on the part of the jaw or a narrowing of the nasal pharynx. Local thickened vowel sounds and white spread vowels are also common. Add to these the tensing of the diaphragm and other breathing muscles when the breath supply or the breath support becomes insufficient, the stiffening of the neck, and the tensing of the legs, and our list is about complete.

All of these interferences result from the effort to "produce the tone" or to make the voice conform to an erroneous concept.

The remedy is found in the development of adequate breath strength, facility in enunciation, freedom in the expressive impulses of the singer and a clear thinking, *musically* accurate mind. Interferences, particularly those of the tongue and jaw, are involuntary compensations for inadequacy of the supporting and controlling functions of breath and posture. The singer who loses breath at the beginning of a phrase, whose rib walls cave in, or whose body slumps in any degree, is marked for compensatory interferences.

Let Go While Holding On

Freedom is possible when the art of "letting go while holding on" has been learned. This important differentiation is the price of freedom in singing. All balance is the result of the pull and resistance of opposite sets of muscles. For example correct posture must be maintained while the lungs are being emptied. The balance which results in control of the breath is the key to the correction of all vocal interferences. Singing uses energy, but should never require effort.

Freeing voices from tension and interferences is usually the first problem the teacher faces. The remedy would seem to be found in a sound foun-

TRAINING THE YOUNG VOICE

ONE OF THE MOST DIFFICULT PROBLEMS IN TRAIN-
ing the young singing voices of America is the
establishment of healthy vocal habits in young people from 11 to 21 years of age. This includes the
years spent in elementary, junior high school,
high school, or the first two college grades. During these years the voices of children pass through
the period of adolescence and become adult.

The *changing voice* of this period remains a
mystery to many who are responsible for the early musical training of young people, even though
some of the best minds in the educational field
have expended a vast amount of research and experience upon it. Leading otolaryngologists advise that the young voice should *rest* from the
moment the change begins, until the voice is *settled*. On the other hand, *educators* point out that
these young people should sing through this period; the surge of energy at this age needs outlet
and boys and girls with changing voices will inevitably talk and shout and scream on the play-

ing fields and in other recreational activity. Proponents of either side of this controversial question can present examples in support of their opposite views. The weight of the majority, however, seems to lean to the side of the educators who have demonstrated over and over that both boys and girls can sing safely through adolescence. It is the absence of competent guidance of young voices that presents the greatest problem. Thorough and safe training in the guidance of young voices is rare in the teaching staffs of elementary and secondary schools.

Adequate vocal training is not generally required of music education majors in our universities, colleges and conservatories. There is, rather, a tendency to require a smattering of instrumental training also. Even when voice training is included in the entire four year course, it is still only one half of that required of a voice major. In other words, the music teacher in the above named schools is at best only half trained to understand the voice. There are some high schools who engage teachers who give individual or small class attention to the problems of the changing voice, but they are few. Where such a fortunate situation exists, the junior high school and the last two elementary grades are still sensitive areas in which competent guidance is rare.

Vocal Abuses of the Young Voice

There are teachers who crowd the young voices for volume. Others will go so far as to expect young voices to sing music that requires sustaining capacity of the vocal mechanism far beyond that which is possible at the tender ages from 13 to 18. Students are taught to open their mouths

102

wide. In response they often close the throat and stiffen the jaw. Operatic music is dangerously improper while the vocal organs are growing rapidly and are therefore physically soft or loose in texture. Overly soft singing encourages devitalization which is not desirable. It is at this age that habits are formed which often last throughout life.

The speech forms, or more specifically, the phonetics of the type of language used in the area in which the student lives, the dialects and speech habits of the environment in which the child grows up will have a profound effect upon his vocal habits. The cultural level of his family and social background will have their effect, and these influences will often add to the problem of the teachers responsible for early musical training. The rapidly growing boy or girl presents postural problems and needs to understand natural breathing.

The Turmoil Within

In addition to the physical changes that take place during puberty, the mental and emotional life is also at a most sensitive and impressionable stage or development. It is at this age that the craving for status appears. The growing young man or woman does not understand the turmoil that goes on within him, but educators should.

Two forms of growing individuality stand out. One is the tendency to hero worship. This often takes the form of breaking with established convention. The thirst for independence appears as a craze for a Sinatra or an Elvis Presley, or a desire for more freedom such as staying out later at night and other escapes from parental supervision. This is the time they need most to be understood for they do not understand themselves.

To those who like music of any kind, amusement expressed about their changing voices is embarrassing and injurious. In their schools they should find that voice changes have been expected and are provided for. In the elementary grades unison and two part singing can be safely used if the pitch range has been kept within comfortable limits.

At all times during the adolescent years the most valuable and attractive asset of the child voice should be maintained; that is, its effortlessness and simplicity. No matter how far the vocal training goes, this remains as a most valuable asset.

The progress of the young voice through an easy comfortable scale can be achieved if there is care to keep the changing voice within its comfortable range limits. These limits may change rapidly. The treble voice is usually most brilliant for about a year before the changing process begins. As it grows heavier or cloudy a quick change to the alto section is advisable. Even allowing a change to either part depending upon the demands of the composition has been found helpful. The S A B music used in the early years of the changing voice soon grows into an S A T B pattern as the age advances.

The Boy's Voice Range

At this point personal direction is advised. The boy's voice should be guided by a competent instructor, who will experiment with the volume or breath pressure, and the vowel sound which responds with the greatest ease. The pitch range can be increased gradually, always avoiding strain, and always patiently assuring the boy that either some vowel form or volume will work.

No Voice Breaks

The chief point to recognize is that no voice really *breaks*. The change may be very evident in some male voices and even in some female voices, but physiologically speaking nothing worthy of the word *break* happens. Just as the body expands and grows taller, so the vocal cords lengthen and thicken by degrees. As the development proceeds, the teacher should place much value on the simplicity, the ease and the pleasure that can be found in singing. The sensitive emotional nature should be fed with ideals of word values, of musical beauty, the pride of achievement and the growing of personal importance.

Music appreciation should be introduced, not for its fame possibilities or monetary value, but as a mark of culture and distinction, feeding the hunger for status and respect. Sight singing with emphasis on pitch accuracy, mental alertness, rhythmic and time values should be pointed out as a valuable accomplishment.

Above all, the young student must be regarded as an individual, not merely as a member of a chorus or glee club. Childlikeness is desirable; it is angelic, but childishness need not be tolerated. Children will obey the kind of discipline which respects them as persons, but will rebel when they are treated as only one of a group.

Vocal Instruction for Music Education Majors Essential

Published works of proper material are plentiful. Vocal instruction for music education majors needs to be spelled out in more specific detail.

Every voice will change, but no voice needs to be ruined or abused. Our especially talented adolescent should never be exploited, either by parents or school. Thus our American heritage of fine voices may be fully realized.

Because the boy's voice seems to drop an octave during the change, teachers have most of their difficulty with the male voice. The safe and easy compass for boys in seventh, eighth and ninth grades is so limited that books of adequate material must be chosen carefully. In these grades the voices of boys fall into six categories: first and second soprano, first and second alto, first and second bass. The tenor voice develops later, and there are few sopranos in this age group. Interchangeability in these parts is usually advisable, because few classifications remain static, even for a semester.

Mabelle Glenn, who has published a Glee Club Book for boys, says, "The voices of boys of junior high school age fall into four divisions: soprano, alto, alto-tenor or cambiata and bass. In all these classifications unison singing, as well as part singing is advisable. A number of communities have organized boy choirs under civic sponsorship, who follow this pattern: Dayton, Ohio; Tulsa, Oklahoma; Columbus, Ohio and others.

At this early stage the teacher becomes aware of the phenomenon of registers and that there is a difference in sound at the various levels of the pitch range. Instructive vowel modification and the natural function of the voice should be allowed to point the way.

106

VOCAL HEALTH

A SINGER, MORE THAN ANY OTHER MUSICIAN, MUST keep his instrument in the best condition possible. The principles of vocal health are equally important to actor, clergyman, teacher, politician or salesman. Anyone who makes his living by the use of his voice finds himself working under the same laws of nature as the singer.

Many take the health of the vocal instrument for granted and forget how ofen we have heard of people who have the misfortune of losing their voices. There was a time when vocal volume and range were considered to be of such importance that all other values were sacrificed for them.

The voice is subject to extremely delicate influences. Its condition at any given moment is affected and determined by physical, mental, emotional and nervous variations. One who uses his voice a great deal must have excellent basic health, and a bit more than usual physical vitality.

Most people subject themselves to vocal abuse while speaking, particularly when under emotional strain, or so neglect the need for adequate rest or sensible eating habits that they invite many conditions detrimental to good singing.

They do these things unintentionally of course, but it must be admitted that the fine edge of vitality and well being in the vocal mechanism so necessary to good singing is rarely found in the average person.

The teachers in the Golden Age of Song, the famous *Bel-Canto* period left us very little in the way of instructive writings. But in the meager records we have of the period, we find much emphasis laid upon rest, exercise and diet. Adding this information to the advice of the medical profession of today, we are told that the body thrives or suffers damage by the nature of what it takes in or gives out.

This is not said facetiously. I mean that the body takes in what it breathes, eats or drinks; and the effects of temperature and humidity must also be taken into account.

The body gives out vocal sound in a manner which either uses the voice in a healthy manner or abuses it. The way the voice is used while either singing or speaking improves or harms it. Its condition does not stand still.

Before considering these two points in further detail, the importance of general health should be stressed. This naturally includes a way of life that provides regular and adequate rest, peace of mind, and the relaxation and sense of general well-being that indicates freedom from neurotic or adverse psychogenic influences. Singing is for victorious, well integrated people. It is for all who are vocally talented of course, but those who are constantly the victims of outer or inner disturbances, find it difficult.

Diet

Diet was a principal preoccupation of the early singing masters. Their suggestions often seem ludicrous in the light of present knowledge, but they went so far as to say, "Physically we are what we eat."

Today we know the benefits of a balanced diet, and we know why eating too much or too little has discernible physical effects. We know also that eating oily, greasy, richly spiced or an excessive amount of starchy foods encourages too much mucous secretion. Also that eating rich foods taxes the digestive system and invites the singer's arch enemy, obesity.

The advice of one prominent health counsellor is that every adult should drink at least six glasses of water a day, in addition to his intake of other liquids such as milk, tea or coffee.

The Effect of Alcoholic Beverages

The use of alcoholic beverages presents an entirely different problem. Practically all singers agree that the use of alcohol before or during a singing engagement is definitely harmful.

One of the old writers refers to alcohol as a "stimulant." It is a mistake to think of alcohol as a stimulant. It is a depressant. It dilates the capillaries and blood vessels and tends to relax the parts that should be under effective control. Full mastery of the voice is thus lost; delicate muscles tend to loosen, and when such loosening

109

becomes chronic, the voice soon becomes hoarse, rough and sluggish.

Some have argued that a drink or two releases them from inhibitions and gives them a sense of freedom. If emotional "looseness" and impairment of control are to be regarded as freedom, perhaps they are right. Franz Alexander says, "Alcohol is the universal solvent of the superego." But who could possibly have more use for his "superego" than one who must appear in public, perform feats of skill, give expression to the most sensitive values, and impress the magnetism of his personality upon those who see and hear him?

But if one suffers from taut nerves or tension, it may be due to fear caused by a lack of preparation. A well prepared artist may feel "keyed up" before a public performance, but if he is really ready and in reasonably good health, he has nothing to fear. "Nerves" and stage fright are misnomers for inadequate experience, mental uncertainty, or emotional immaturity. It is possible to use an alcoholic beverage without immediate harm, but its continued use over a long period is sure to be injurious.

The Importance of Fresh Air

Nothing can take the place of good fresh air. The heated air in the rooms in which most people in northern climates live is all too often dry and dehumidified. Humidity gauges are now easily obtainable. When the relative humidity in a room is reduced to as little as 20%, steps should be taken to restore it to a 35 to 40% level. Otherwise, the efficiency of that wonderful air conditioning mechanism, the nose and the throat, may be impaired. Electrical appliance stores and medical supply houses now furnish easily operated means to control humidity. Dryness of the mucous membrane of the nose and throat, often the result of low humidity, should be avoided.

The mucosa protecting the turbinates—cone-shaped sections of the walls of the nasal cavity—are covered by microscopic hairs called cilia. It is the function of the cilia to weave back and forth and thereby to move the mucus to the back of the nose and into the throat, where it is swallowed. Dust and dirt inhaled through the mouth will tend to move upward to the back of the mouth to be disposed of in the same manner.

Thus it will be seen that nature has provided a marvelous mechanism for the protection of the glottis, vocal cords, windpipe and the bronchi.

The air inhaled is also warmed to the temperature of these parts. That is the reason why breathing frigid air through the mouth should be avoided. Conversation on the street in below zero weather is not recommended. If the whole body can be affected by radical temperature changes, how much more that is true of the more delicate structures of the larynx and trachea.

Clothing

Clothing is another important item in the adjustment of the body to radical changes in temperature. While chilling should be avoided, dressing too warmly and coddling the body is more likely to weaken resistance to infection. Dressing lightly enough so that the skin can perform its function of adjustment to temperature changes is, fortunately, becoming more general practice. Even so, medical men feel that women, as a rule, wear too little and men wear too much. However, individual tolerance is always a factor. Between the "fresh air fiend" and the overly sensitive person who is never comfortable unless he is in an overheated room, the singer should find a balance best adapted to his personal degree of tolerance.

Fumes and Dust

Strong chemical fumes are also harmful, especially when one is exposed to them over long periods. Places where such chemicals (such as paints) are manufactured, or where they are used in a manufacturing process, present a danger to the singing voice.

Another injurious factor is fine dust. We are all familiar with the protective masks worn by those who work with cement or other commercial products in powdered form, and with the masks worn by doctors and nurses in hospitals to protect them from germs. Sometimes we are not alert to the fact that house dust, or dust encountered while cleaning a basement, or dust blown about in the street, can also have an irritating effect upon the delicate membranes of the vocal mechanism.

The Effects of Smoking

Teachers and physicians are often asked, "Does smoking harm the throat?" The picture is not too clear at this writing, but there is certainly adequate evidence to prove that smoking does harm to one's general health. The case against nicotine is negligible. Other factors in the smoke itself, such as the tars and heat, do the real harm.

Regardless of the form in which tobacco is

smoked, cigar, cigarette, or pipe, the oral cavity, pharynx, and nasal passages are exposed to harmful tars, resins, and heat. When the smoke is inhaled, as it is by most cigarette smokers and occasionally by others, the delicate structures of the voice box and the bronchi are subjected directly to this deleterious influence.

Smoke from any source is injurious and should be avoided. My own experience with singers who have stopped smoking has been to note immediate improvement in clarity of voice, texture of skin and hair, and to some extent digestive organs. The recent discussions about the influence of smoking upon lung cancer we will leave to the realm of the physician and interested persons.

Incorrect Use of Vocal Organs

The chief threat to vocal well-being is abuse of the vocal organs through wrong use. Sometimes faulty speech habits establish a pattern that can be sustained only by great pressure and strain. Singers frequently get into trouble by trying to make the voice sound as they think it should, rather than letting it function freely. By singing naturally they often find their best quality through expressive motivation instead of physical sensation.

Striving for more extended pitch range or greater vocal power invariably induces fatigue in a vocal mechanism not yet developed enough to endure so much effort. Many students in their practice will sing "too high too long." A tenor of my acquaintance said once, "A tenor will never get anywhere without a good A natural or a B flat." His practice periods consisted entirely of testing his ability to sing these notes. If his A or B flat were "there" his day was made. If it were not, his day was ruined. A singer who forces his voice, either for range or volume, will soon find himself in serious trouble. A too insistent salesman who talks too loudly or too much will experience periods of hoarseness, as will school teachers who do not sustain a resonant line in the school room, and who are subject to feelings of tension.

Range and power are by-products of good singing. They never have to be sought for in themselves. Crooning was popular for a time until its exponents found that this disturbance of natural balance in the vocal adjustment ruined their voices.

Singers who must sing when physically exhausted are in special danger. Unfortunate results to the vocal mechanism will be encountered by those who sing too soon after an illness. The musical comedy star who has eight performances a week and frequent extra rehearsals, or a night-club singer singing five or six hours a night, with recording sessions during the day, also courts vocal disaster. So, also, does a singer recovering from pneumonia or influenza, who might find even rehearsals of a taxing opera role or a principal part in a stage production so tiring that compensatory patters are often formed which result either in a limitation of range or a permanent change in voice quality.

The Common Cold

The common "cold" frequently interrupts a singer's work schedule. The "cold" may often result in secondary effects such as laryngitis, pharyngitis and influenza. The only self-treatment for a "cold" which has the sanction of the physician, is rest in bed, a light diet, and abundant intake of fluids. The only gargle that is approved is hot salt water. The salt acts as a cleanser of the tissues contacted, but the infection is usually where no gargle can touch it. Aspirin in moderate amounts has some acceptance, but the fact is emphasized that it is a palliative to relieve the discomfort rather than a cure.

The real danger is from the "secondary invaders." This is often avoided if the patient will spend a day or two in bed, especially while there is any evidence of fever. When engorged vocal cords, "strep" throat or bronchial involvement are suspected, a physician should be called in immediately. Neglect or self treatment of these conditions is perilous. Modern medicine is well equipped to cope with such conditions and advice of a competent physician should be followed to the letter. The future of the voice may be at stake.

The "Forced" Voice

But still, the most frequent cause of vocal disorder is forcing the voice through a constricted throat. In the quest for vocal intensity and carrying power, this condition occurs more frequently than we like to think. The resulting nodules, hoarseness, weakness and aphonia must be placed in the hands of the physician and the vocal therapist for correction. Chronic hoarseness, post-nasal drip, sinus infections, and similar difficulties are usually correctable when placed in proper hands. It should be understood, however, that the physician and the vocal therapist are two different people; both have important parts to play if vocal oblivion is to be avoided. The physician deals with

115

infections and such other physical problems as polyps, cleft palate, deviation of septum, adenoids, etc. The most illuminating work on this subject to come before the public in recent years, is a book called *Keep Your Voice Healthy* by Dr. Friedrich Brodnitz, published by Harper & Brothers in 1953.

Dr. Brodnitz presents the physician's point of view and gives names and addresses of authorities in Vocal Therapy.* The latter deals with the causes of vocal difficulties and works to correct them.

*George A. Kopp, Secretary, American Speech and Hearing Association, Wayne University, Detroit, Michigan.
*G. L. Wyatt, *The Chewing Approach to Voice Therapy,* International Science Publishing Co., 250 Fifth Avenue, New York, New York.
*Deso A. Weiss, *The Chewing Approach to Speech and Voice Therapy,* S. Karger, New York, New York.

The profession of Vocal Therapy is comparatively new, but it is making an important place for itself in a world where the use of the voice is becoming more important. The field is concerned with such areas as loss of voice from post-operative conditions and physical abnormalities. But the most illuminating part of the work of the vocal therapist is the detection of vocal strain in clergymen who address large audiences with the voice of authority or persuasion, or in salesmen who speak with insistent enthusiasm, or in the politicians who make several speeches each night without previous vocal training. Others will also benefit from such treatment: the actor who must use his voice in seven to nine performances a week while under constant nervous strain, and the young mother who is continually calling to her children in the fear that they might be hurt by various mechanical items in our society.

When the nervous tension under which many people use their voices is considered, it is surprising that our voices survive as well as they do, and equally surprising that we as teachers of singing have been so tardy in emphasizing the need for saner living, saner voice use, and recognition of the importance of corrective vocal therapy.

Ages ago in ancient Rome, the phrase was coined *mens sana in corpore sano* — a healthy mind is to be found only in a healthy body. Let us paraphrase it for those whom we teach — *vox sana in corpore sano*. And let us impress our students with its truth and its importance so that they may never lose sight of the need for healthful living. I believe we shall be better teachers for it.

MUSICIANSHIP

THE KEY TO THE ABILITY TO SING IS NOT IN THE voice alone, but also in musicianship. Without this the performer in any medium is like a blind man groping in the dark.

Musicianship is musical knowledge and skill based upon the talent of innate musicality. It involves all the separate singing skills, and with them a complete co-ordination that integrates mind, eye, ear, and voice into one single precision instrument.

Singing belongs in the field of applied music. It assumes thorough knowledge of the fundamentals of music, and the developed skill to perform it. It is subject to the same principles that govern performance on the piano, the violin or any other instrument.

Good performance demands not only adequate musical education, but also the re-creation of the original inspiration of the composer. A sensitive musician will interpret every nuance, every variation of tempo, and every point of musical emphasis in a song, as well as the meaning of its text.

Of course one must know music. A singer is fortunate indeed if he became familiar with it as a child, if he learned some instrument before he started to sing. Some lucky artists have spent all their years saturated in music. The singer who approaches his career without a musical background has a double task. It may even be triple: he may have to learn to speak properly as well as to learn music and acquire a vocal technique.

When young people go to a singing teacher for an honest appraisal it is not their vocal equipment alone that he judges. Along with a healthy throat the promising singer must have a feeling for musical effect. Vocal development usually means that the singer takes the voice he has and uses it properly. If he then finds that he has a beautiful voice, so much the better—that is an extra dividend. But beauty of the voice is due to a gift for expressive effect more often than to physical endowment.

Musicianship comes first. Mr. Frederick W. Root thought that artistic interpretation is like a statue supported by four pillars: musical knowledge, voice development, facility of execution and diction.

Sight Singing

A violinist spares no effort to become a good musician, but there are some singers (yes, even celebrated ones) who are quite helpless when faced by a bit of new music. This will not do. One must learn to read music *at sight,* however much practice it requires. Rehearsals and mass production methods are expensive nowadays, and sight reading is a *must*. It is an advantage to learn to play an instrument, but the Italian method of studying solfege is the better method. Then intervals, time values and rhythm patterns receive balanced attention.

Application

One must study "how to study". Professor Whitehead said that it takes an unusual mind to examine the obvious; so also it takes an unusual singer to pay full attention to small details. Herein lies greatness. As Michelangelo said: trifles make perfection, and perfection is no trifle.

Every musical composition has a plan. It is necessary to know the designs of ballad, art song, word picture, oratorio or opera. Then as they are sung, each phrase, while a unit in itself, fills its place in the song or aria as a whole.

Background

It is necessary to know song styles; to recognize and treat appropriately the difference among popular, classic and romantic types of music—as well as the dramatic music of opera and stage, and the devout music of the church.

Musicianship is the primary requisite of the profession. Listen to others sing, especially the successful artists. Listen to the great orchestras, pianists, violinists and performers of chamber music. Much may be learned that way.

Study musical history, especially the history of vocal music. The better the different musical eras are understood, the more fully the singer is equipped to present his songs and arias.

Self Discipline

Experience has taught me that before a person can master music, he must learn to master himself. Self-control or self-mastery is a state of being. He must *feel* like an efficient musical instrument.

Keep the vocal instrument healthy and vital. Work always at improving musical taste and sensitivity. A tone sounds different to the singer than to the listener, because a singer hears himself by bone induction, while the listener hears with his ears. For this reason the singer should make what use he can of recording machines. But still, intonation and tone quality depend above all upon his anticipatory hearing.

Training of the Ear

Musical education centers primarily on ear training. Pitch intonation is followed by systematic drill in the study of intervals. Then key relationships, modulations from key to key, and scales must be mastered.

Musicianship means being able to interpret a musical mood. We have long used "the happy little thought within" — the artificial yet spontaneous joyous mood — as one of our vocal devices. There are other moods, too. Truly appreciating the mood involves understanding the musical meaning. Its first consideration is tempo. The tempo of most standard music is determined by tradition; any breaks with such tradition must be strongly justified. Then there is rhythm, that regularly recurring pulse which is the secret of aliveness in music. It is the adhesive that holds phrases together and enables the singer to present his song as a whole. Young singers should

121

strive to appreciate this, for it is a weak point with many of them.

Continuity

No good singing artist will permit a phrase to "sit down," or "fall down," while he detaches himself during an instrumental interlude. Remember what Plunkett Greene said: "Never stop the march of a song. Sing mentally through the rests."

Dynamics is one of the major musical devices. This is where vocal flexibility counts. The capacity to swell and diminish without loss of tone or intensity is a great test of vocal technique. A tone which is static in volume is in danger of becoming monotonous. Some singers lack sufficient variety of dynamic pressure to make their singing flexible, others tend to overdo extreme effects. Every song must be as definite in dynamic pattern as in pitch pattern.

There are too many other devices of musical expression for me to even mention them all. Accent, stressed and unstressed parts of a phrase, pressure marks, staccato and the newer devices being presented by modern composers — let these remind us that we have resources of expressive mechanics to implement the most fertile imagination.

I can sympathize with those who find the elusive elements of tone production difficult, but not with those who go on for years deficient in musicianship. Of course, the singer's musical education often starts late; and in some ways he does have to create and build his own instrument. But he must aim at winning the respect of instrumentalists instead of confirming those who delight in emphasizing the difference between "singers" and "musicians."

Musical Skill

Acquiring musical skill is a laborious task. But though the heights are still beyond us, the next step is always a simple one. Keep on, taking one step at a time. Lack of musical feeling is the reef on which many an ambition has been wrecked. Opportunities to strengthen this element are present all around us. Classes in theory for singers are easy to find. Participate in ensembles whenever possible. Choir and chorus work are the best media for drill known, and they are constantly open to those who desire musical skill earnestly enough to go to trouble.

Study Piano?

Must a singer learn to play the piano? It is not essential but advisable. He must be able to read music at sight. There are no black and white keys in the throat. The singer must think pitch, and calculate the distance from one note to another. Sight singing, together with keen observation while singing much vocal music, will result in the ability to "think" pitch independently of any other instrument or voice. It is very useful to study harmony, but the real point is that at the sight of music the singer must be able to hear it mentally. This capacity comes from practice in classes, patient drill, and alert attention to what one is doing.

When learning a new song or aria, the singer should first become familiar with the text, and play the music a few times on the piano. Then he should sing it and co-ordinate the eye and ear. He cannot "learn a song with the throat." He must think of the intervals and time values. Difficulties must be figured out; the piano cannot do the pitch thinking for him.

The singer must understand all styles of music. Arias from great oratorios, or from Italian, French or German operas, all have different styles of expression. The same is true of art songs, folk songs, ballads, impressionistic word pictures or contemporary music. Popular songs of our present day also have a style all their own.

The great secret of musicianship is this: *prepare, prepare*. Be ready for opportunity when it comes. If lack of musicianship is the obstacle, it is removable *now*.

SONG STYLES

AFTER THE SINGER HAS BEEN SINGING FOR A WHILE, he will find his various songs, arias or roles falling quite naturally into a few separate and recognizable categories.

Interpretation is the art of translating or of reincarnating the original ideas of the poet and composer. Each of the various song styles should be interpreted by the performer in such a manner that the original inspiration becomes the immediate experience of the listener.

A study of the history of monody, or the writing of the music in a single line as for the solo voice, is absolutely necessary for any singer who wishes to be recognized as an artist.

The beginnings of music for the solo voice are found with the Minnesingers of Germany, and the Troubadours of France and Italy in the 11th to the 13th centuries. These artists continued for many years thereafter. We must acknowledge the vocal art of the early days of vocal history, but this has little value or interest here.

In the period from the 14th to the 16th centuries the only people with any appreciable degree of learning or culture were the clergy and the aristocracy. The music and poetry they created were created for its own sake, with beauty of form its object rather than depth of content.

Beginning of Opera and Oratorio

In about 1550 a group of men in Florence known as the Camerata (the courtiers of Count Bardi) met frequently to study the old Greek Drama. In the effort to revive it they developed the recitative, which made musical dialogue or recitation possible. Combining this new form with the solo music they already knew, they brought *opera seria* into being. *Opera buffa,* or comic opera, followed soon after and both styles grew and flourished in Italy.

The oratorio, beginning about 1600, was a presentation of sacred subjects, a kind of continuation of the *mysteries* and *miracle plays* that had been a part of church life, but without the secularization and abuses that had crept into them. Caccini in Italy, and Heinrich Schutz in Germany were leaders among those who set the style of oratorio as we know it today.

The Baroque Period

About 1600 the Baroque period appeared. The spirit of Baroque was extravagant and fantastic as compared to the previous century. It was expressed in the architecture, the painting and the music. Everything was expected to be large and noble. Here we find the grandeur that was Handel and the glory of Bach. It was heard in the operatic music of Monteverdi and is generally considered to end with Handel's death in 1759.

This was not the only characteristic of this paradoxical period. It also saw the birth of the age of reason. There was an effort to understand the world in terms of logic and rational clarity. It was an age when form was considered above content. It brought forth the music known to singers as the early Italian Classics. A contemporary of Monteverdi was Purcell in England. Clarity and simplicity of expression govern the style, with strict regard for the principle of orderly sequence. Singers will recognize the *A, B, A,* form of this epoch. A song or aria would have a strong melodious first theme, followed by a contrasted, gentler second theme in another key, and then a return to the first theme ending in the original key.

The Rococo Period

In the early eighteenth century the Rococo period appeared. This was a product of court life where few were serious or intellectual. It was given to elaboration, delicacy and fine detail. Everything was in miniature and elegance, and big things were considered rather vulgar. Its best remembered exponents are Couperin (1668-1733) and Pergolesi (1710-1736), though some of Bach's secular music belongs to that period also. Not much of this vocal music is still in use.

The Romantic Period

The classic style flows through the music of Haydn and Mozart, but a revolt against the confines of classicism was inevitable. "Hinaus ins Freue" meaning literally "Away from here into the open" was first spoken by Goethe in *Faust* and soon taken up by Schiller, Rousseau, Byron, and in music by the mighty Beethoven.

19th century romanticism gave us music of the people; it was inspired by human emotions rather than form, personal instead of purely intellectual.

There were many composers in this era, and their music was rich in content. Here we find the composers Liszt, Chopin, Mendelssohn, Schubert, Schumann, Brahms and many others and a culmination of the period in the music of Richard Strauss.

Tschaikowsky, Grieg and Sibelius are examples of the composers whose music followed definite nationalistic traits, as did indeed the music of Brahms.

Impressionism

The impressionism of Debussy, and the French style of Fauré, Ravel and Poulenc are too near our own time to need historic explanation here. This is also true of the moderns such as Schonberg, Hindemith, Stravinsky and other contemporary composers. The vital point to be made is that valid interpretation of any music must be founded upon familiarity with its origin in time, person and place, whether that be 16th or 19th century, or the composer Monteverdi, Mozart, Schumann or Gershwin.

To interpret well we must know more than one example of the style of music we sing. Each period and each composer has many sides, as a jewel has many facets. A single song of Brahms or Strauss is not enough to give us the feeling we *know* the composer. The repertoire of an accomplished singer must be very extensive, even though he limit himself to one style as the lieder singers did. This is what background and preparation means, and it applies as much to modern popular music as to the music of the masters.

The study of interpretation is an intellectual responsibility on the part of the singing artist, but the *act* is an expression of the emotional reactions it arouses in him. It is just because this response is different in each artist that we are willing and glad to hear the same works performed over and over by different artists. In the hands of each it is ever new. The song or aria may belong for all time to its composer, but its interpretation belongs to the singer himself, and by the quality and impact of that interpretation he succeeds or fails as an artist.

If you ever heard John Charles Thomas sing the little French song in which he impersonates a sleepy little girl, you will remember how he expressed sleepiness by singing a quarter of a tone flat. Tibbett did the same thing when he sang a song by Hughes called *Bricklayer Love*. Disgust, discouragement and a feeling of being tired of it all was unmistakable. In contrast, beauty makes its own demands. Lotte Lehmann in her delightfully poetic Schubert songs and Jennie Tourel in her deliciously flavored French chansons always made the listener feel the inner meaning of the text.

Interpretation uses attitude, tone coloring, and appropriate pronunciation of words as a skillful mechanic uses the tools of his trade. We do these things all the time when we speak. Whether we are aware of it or not, we express interest, indifference, alarm or contentment by the way we pronounce words. This is what "sing as you speak," (a suggestion often heard in the vocal

129

studios) really means. It means sing with the same cadences, the same word enunciation and articulation that we use in speech, and the same size and percussive value of vowels and consonants. But it does not mean that the singer should use the over-relaxed level which is often employed in speaking.

Singing with verbal and vocal response to meaning, especially if that meaning is poetic, amounts to vocal acting, or doing with pronunciation and voice what we might also do with posture and gesture. The singer runs the risk of becoming so absorbed in his own vocal musical experience that he gives his audience nothing to which it can respond. The listener quickly becomes tired of such a voice. The audience wants to respond to the meaning of the words.

Dynamics quickly convey emotion. The art of shaping a phrase so that it fits perfectly into the pattern of the whole song, is a test of both emotional and vocal flexibility. The ability to create atmosphere and to attract a feeling response on the part of the listener must be learned, so that interpretations may have maturity and authority.

Until this is achieved, success may elude the singer. The public realizes that the artist lacks something, and he is often accused of not having enough experience. This is a demanding art. It will reward the singer who expands and demonstrates intelligence, work and patience, but it will not reduce its demands. The public knows the difference between the excellent and the mediocre performance.

Fine interpretation must include those subjective qualities in a person that cannot be measured or named. Obviously, skill in the techniques of voice, musicianship, language and personal presentation underlie all effective performance. But what is felt, though not consciously seen, is the total response of the whole person, the over-all effect produced by the inner artist.

A good interpreter must possess imagination. The poet and the composer have given him outlines; he must fill them in with living substance. His song must first be alive with his life, made understandable by his own intelligence, and life-like by the contributions of his own emotions.

The song has been in existence since it was composed. It is brought into the living *now* by the life and feeling of the interpreter. He did not create it, but he brings it into conscious being again by recreating it. That is his function, and the more effectively and truthfully he can do it, adding, meanwhile, the force of his own creativity, the better artist he proves himself to be.

Completeness of self-expression is a joy that few people know, believe it or not. It is one of the most delightful, rewarding and satisfying experiences in life, and life has very few fully satisfying moments for most people. Singers, singing from their very souls, are nearer to it than most people. If they have the good fortune to feel such a moment of release, they should savor it. They should seek it, work for it, and taste a joy that is greater than money or fame.

Need for Authority

If vocal performance is going to have strength, it must have that quality of authority that comes from a thorough grasp and understanding of all the subtle shades of meaning hidden in the subject matter. Convincing interpretation imposes a double obligation. The singer must develop mental qualities of appreciation, sensitiveness of feeling and a capacity for response, on the one hand, and a thorough and penetrating understanding of his musical material on the other. Even where conspicuous talent is present, an extensive education and a complete emotional awakening may still be needed.

The Final Use

Finally we come to that moment when we stand before the public. Then our measure is taken by our capacity to interest people. This is the crux of the whole matter. People want to be interested. They hope to be moved, to have their feelings touched. They hope to be fascinated and swept on to the point of being thrilled. It doesn't happen often; for such an experience, on the part of both audience and performer, depends on so many unpredictable attributes. One who sings beautifully needs, in addition, to arouse a soul satisfying emotional effect in his listeners. This may be done by following a few basic principles:

1. The ability to lose all sense of self and to lose it in the complete service of what he does.
2. To be fully and completely aware of the *inner* meaning of each word of the text, of the musical line that expresses it, and in control of all the devices of expression. These will include word emphasis, tone color, dynamics and facial expression—and all of the emotional and personality qualities necessary to graphic translation and expression.
3. The ability to present the performance in an attractive package is also important. This is appearance, and that inner calm that never

lets one's own feelings interfere with the mechanics of expression. It means all the elements of style, stage deportment and eloquence of manner. It means self-presentation carried to the point of skill.

Emotional control while singing in public is indispensable. The artist who is the victim of his own self-consciousness or fear is not prepared to perform in public. Emotional maturity implies the capacity to channel emotions appropriately, and at will. Otherwise, public performance is disturbed by personal reactions, or the belief that a singer must arouse the emotions of his listeners by the over-display of his own.

I am satisfied that many of the world's renowned artists of today would be singing even if their art had not won general acceptance. If they are born singers ,they must sing to live, or otherwise die of bitterness and frustration.

Beautiful singing is only partially dependent upon acceptance by the public. It is an expression of the individual, which is the result of his own genius.

The fortunate singer is one who so passionately loves to sing that he risks anything and everything to fully express what he feels. This is why the capacity to feel must be so constantly fed and encouraged. This is why only the person who can feel knows how to sing. And only the person who feels and sings in terms of his listener will grip and hold his listener's attention. We call this *empathy*—the ability to project the content of the soul into the soul of another being.

This is it, then. He must sing in terms of the consciousness of the listener and with a full and adequate grasp of what he has to say.

INTERPRETATION

To win and hold the attention of an audience, to magnetize feeling until the electric current of intimate communication is established— then to satisfy that feeling of expectancy to the point where it is ready to burst with enthusiasm: that is showmanship.

Among its requisites are vocal effectiveness, attractive appearance, technical proficiency and command of the type of music used.

The singer may either be born with beauty of voice and a flair for performance, or he may have cultivated these qualities by concentrated attention and practice; in any case, they are wasted talents if not accompanied by technical proficiency. Technique of some kind is the foundation of skill in the performance of anything, and in nothing is this so obviously true as in music. Well directed study, application, determination and perseverance will be needed before it is realized.

Gifted singers who have not taken the trouble to learn their business are all around us. The popular trend to exploit *talent* and to cash in on its appeal during early youth has destroyed the possibility of a lucrative career for many a potential artist.

The Foundation of Vocal Technique

The foundation of all vocal technique is breath control. While singing a beautiful phrase, what could be more disconcerting, more destructive to composure and poise than the sudden realization that one is running out of breath. Or what could more effectively impair the beauty of the voice than those involuntary compensatory tensions of jaw and tongue and throat caused by lack of adequate control?

Many singers are quite satisfied with their breathing capacities until they meet the demands for virtuosity found in oratorios such as those by Handel's *Messiah,* Brahm's *Requiem,* Bach's *B Minor Mass,* or in standard opera arias. Many songs are beyond the capacities of singers with the voice to sing them until breath control has been realized, and capacity for opera requires development far beyond the equipment of average singers. It is found only in the few who live with singleness of purpose and faithful devotion. An inspired sincere artist commands respect and attention. Success follows.

Vocal Freedom

Freedom of tonal emission also meets many a test. From the top to the bottom of the voice range, ability to sing in response to interpretative intention is in constant demand. Compromise, made necessary by inadequacy in any part of the vocal range, leaves the expressive powers limited in capacity.

Flexibility and Intonation

Flexibility of voice is also important. The test of vocal tone is often found in a singer's dynamic range. Most singers can crescendo even if it takes some effort, but the ability to diminish in volume to the vanishing point in all parts of the pitch range is not to be taken for granted. And it should never be forgotten that such vocal effectiveness depends upon vocal ease. Important and difficult as these technical elements are, they must seem easy to the listener.

Intimacy

Accuracy of intonation, simplicity and naturalness in the enunciation of words and absolute certainty and security of musicianship are among the *musts* for effective performance. The singer cannot feel that he is effective until he has established an intimacy with his audience that makes them feel he is taking them into his confidence.

These freedoms are held at a high price. Even when they seem to be the accident of talent they do not remain so. Sometime, sooner or later these techniques must be mastered. An acceptable substitute for skill has never yet been discovered.

Familiarity With Musical Idiom

In the field of musical ability there must be complete certainty and familiarity with that musical structure which is being performed at the moment, and the entire background from which

136

it springs. This is equally true of the operatic or concert star, or the singer of popular songs. Musical certainty is more than knowing notes, intervals, time and rhythm patterns. It is knowing what the music is intended to say and the language or idiom in which it must be said.

This is a field of study where preparation must reflect devotion and purpose. It is the reason behind the study of repertoire. There can be no freedom of interpretation and, therefore, no showmanship where uncertainty, lack of discernment or lack of familiarity with the material presented exists.

Every song the singer sings should be only one of a number of its kind that he knows. Security in technique and completely rehearsed musical certainty are the foundations not only of good interpretation, but of vocal freedom as well. Those who are fortunate enough to have had some kind of musical training in their childhood find music less of a problem than those whose acquaintance with it began later in life. Even where there is innate musicality, every step of the way along the road to a musical education must be traversed from its very beginning. In these days when the performances of great artists, leading orchestras and fine musicians have become available through recordings, radio and television, early and formative opportunities are more frequent than they were in former years. The fulfillment of a true musician comes not through acts of doing, but as a state of being. It may have its roots far back in previous generations, but the musicianship which results in personal freedom is a basic musicality plus musical training.

Musicianship and vocal skill complement each

other, so that the voice becomes the vehicle of the meanings found in the music and the words. When the artist has mastered these, his listener finds himself completely in the presence of the poet and the composer, rather than a mere witness to a singer's performance.

Singers who have gained this freedom experience the intimate association of the music, the poetry, the audience, and themselves.

When physiological, musical and verbal techniques are mastered, the artist is able to establish with his audience a sympathetic relationship which releases an abundance of emotional expression. He must pay for this with faithful application combined with persistence.

Magnetism

Magnetism is the power to attract and hold attention until the desired response is achieved. Sound health is its foundation, but it is much more than animal force and vitality. It is the capacity to win the sympathy, the affections, the interest and finally the convictions of one's listeners. To command all this, a singer must feel emotionally bound up in what he does. Emotion attracts, and when an audience feels genuine emotion in a performer, it will be deeply moved by what is called *empathy* or *induction*, with similar emotion.

Losing One's Self

To this end the real showman often projects a personality entirely of his own creation. He formulates an individual who may be an entirely different entity from the conventional person he is in every day life. He plays a role, assuming such personal elements of style as abounding cheerfulness, complete faith in himself and his product; a positive appreciation for and an emotional response in what he sings. He gives free play to his imagination and literally becomes the character for whom he speaks. The audience cannot conceive of the artist as singer Thomas Smith; for the listener the artist *is Mimi, Manon, Lohengrin,* or the poet who originally was inspired to compose the text.

Through this self-created being he interprets all the emotions and the intense feeling he finds in his songs or role. For this reason, he can interpret emotion without becoming too emotional himself, for if he did he would unseat his technique and lose control of his voice.

The Importance of the Eye

His greatest friend is his eye. It must see the vision of that which he is creating. His eye must not rove or seem in the least distracted. Mental concentration and a deliberate use of silences attract attention. Intimate communication upon a mutually sympathetic plane will hold it and defeat the roving eye or the early yawn. He must dispense with his score and sing from memory. He will also find that printed words in the hands of his audience are not his friends.

"Magnetism," says Plunkett Greene, "is the undefinable something which passes from singer to audience, and audience to singer alike, for the audience which the singer holds in the hollow of his hand, holds him as surely in its own. Each acts and reacts upon the other in increasing degree. It is a gossamer thread over which passes that nameless electric current which stirs the singer to his depths and holds the audience thrilled and still."

The Mood

Every song or aria has its mood. The impressiveness of a performance depends upon the degree of emotional vitality with which the artist can charge it. Imagination, and a trained emotional nature are needed to establish a mood sufficiently potent to create atmosphere while holding the attention of a large number of people.

The text of the song will furnish the material for atmosphere, but the mood must be created by the singer. The text should be studied until its significance is fully grasped, not only in terms of what it says, but in what it implies. The singer, in appreciating the expressed and the implied objectives of the composer, should at the same time enter into the proper mood. The mood is an emotional state which colors the voice, influences the facial and other body responses, and is already reflected in the singer's eyes. This is why we say the eyes are magnetism's best friend. They should, however, be sincere and truthful. Artificiality or pretense destroys effectiveness.

Atmosphere is usually an idealized state describing an emotional experience, painting a scene or relating an event. Its presence is felt when that breathless rapport exists between artist and listeners that has been described, "You could hear a pin drop."

The formula for such sympathetic communication has been described by one public performer as faith in himself, unquestioning limitless faith, personal humility and true love for his listener, and because love is the most powerful motivation in the world, all resistance melts before it. Thus one artist has been able to pyramid the results to fabulous proportions.

After admitting the necessity for talent, adequate equipment and technique, this combination of faith in one's self and love for people might well become the recognized formula for success.

Song interpretation is a comprehensive term, including the singer's complete understanding of his material, his relation to the listening public, his elegance and effectiveness of verbal expression, and his complete mastery of himself.

TONE COLOR

TONE COLOR IS THE VOCAL RESPONSE TO FEELING OR
emotion. People who are naturally free in feeling,
will show their response by fleeting changes in
facial or eye expression, in body movement, or in
the tone of the voice.

These subtle changes are usually evident in the
speaking voice. It expresses interest, indifference,
pleasure, disappointment, surprise, anger, tenderness, or 101 other reactions. It does this quite
naturally if there is no fixation or impediment
present.

In singing, the first requisite for tone color is a
free functioning voice that is completely under
control. The voice is then so natural in its expression of feeling that it takes on varying colors
automatically. The next thing needed is an emotional nature, quickly responsive to the feeling
expressed in poetry or drama. Such a nature is
developed by feeding the emotional life freely
with the material of which songs are made.

We frequently forget that a song is a sequence

of events: first an inspiration or emotion, then a poem, and then the music which gives it expression.

When atmosphere and mood have been imaginatively created, tone color will follow easily if the singer's mind and voice are free — free of voice consciousness or any other form of self-consciousness. This is a stage of interpretation that is never reached until there is a perfected technique.

The painter who works with tangible materials, gives careful study to the quality of his colors. "Just paint" will not do. There must be variety and shades of color to express fully the ideas he wishes to appear on canvas.

The singer is more limited in material, for he has only the tone of his voice with which to paint his picture, convey his meaning and move his audience. To do this with just one characteristic tone quality would obviously be as monotonous as painting a landscape in just one tint. Tone color is that mixing of the overtones of the voice, that shaping of the resonance, that variety of tonal form, texture and volume by which different meanings are made clear and convincing to the listener.

Let me emphasize that it is no use to even think about tone color before the mechanics of singing are fully established. The tone must be the natural expression of the singer. This implies a production free and balanced; never stiffly held in a fixed position and form, and never devitalized or spiritless. Too often the singing tone is artificial, the result of imitation of incorrect models, of insecurity in voice or musicianship, or of false concepts of vocal action. When any of these mis-

143

conceptions are present, the true voice of the singer is obscured.

Emotional response on the part of the listener to the singer's tone color is very important. This is especially true in the direct personal songs of the romantic period, the impressionistic *style*, the open sentimentality of the ballad, or the brooding intensity of some of the negro spirituals. Every song has its mood. Plunket Greene said, "The atmosphere belongs to the song, the mood belongs to the singer." There must then be a mood for every song, and a specific mood for every word; and the singer must supply the *appropriate* mood.

The English language is filled with words that, in their very sound, suggest the mood. A word like *touch* with a slight hesitation on the *ch* is highly suggestive. So also, is *sweet, soft, splash,* or *dash, dream* and *home*.

In the study of tone color we find some authorities defining it as, "Sing as you would speak." This means that the sound of the voice is vitalized by the feeling expressed in the word, and that feeling must be free from any limitation if the color is to be consistent and convincing. The quickness with which audiences respond to such expression is one of the greatest joys of the singing artist.

The human voice is the only musical instrument capable of arousing such an effect. All other instruments must depend upon variations of tempo or degrees of intensity or power. The voice possesses the natural capacity for a higher form of expression than is possible with any other instrument which makes music.

PERSONALITY

This chapter is addressed directly to the singer who performs or who is preparing to perform publicly.

SOMETIMES YOU DO YOUR BEST WORK IN PUBLIC when you are impersonating someone else. Something about the character you pretend to be has an ennobling effect upon you. Something of dignity, of stature, that is not a part of you when you play yourself, gets into you and you feel a release of forces within that your personal life never inspires.

Such a thing is *characterization*. It is so much easier to pretend to be someone else, than it is to be yourself with all your fears, inhibitions and limitations. Playing a part gives purpose to your daring, and the need for self-justification disappears.

Professional direction in creative dramatics is extremely useful to the singer. He needs guidance while he discovers how best to use his imaginative

145

powers. He needs encouragement while learning to fully release those powers without over-playing the character he represents.

Characterization is impersonation. It is knowing the motivations, desires, fears and feelings of another person. Preferably it should be an individual with authority and tradition, so that you can attain the release necessary to project yourself into the role completely and thoroughly.

Most people think acting is difficult. It isn't if you rid yourself *of yourself* and create a mood and an atmosphere that is the product of your imagination. Usually costumes, lighting, stage properties and other attributes are there to help you.

Imagination and courage, supported by adequate preparation or experience, are your greatest aids when you are before the public in your own person. When you lose yourself in the mood you create, you may feel that you have exposed your soul, but if your portrayal is sincere, you have nothing to fear.

Characterization is confined almost entirely to the stage and to songs of the romantic period wherein expression is personal and impassioned. In all songs you can let yourself go without fear. There are no fixed rules in self expression. Manner and mannerisms are best when they are pure invention. But they require complete externalization of self.

Singers often find their greatest problems in the field of personal presentation. The mastery of vocal, musical and verbal techniques is not beyond the reach of those with an appreciable degree of talent and intelligence, but in the final analysis, the song is presented in terms of the personality of the performer.

What personality is, in all its aspects, can best be explained by the professional psychologists, but, as singers and teachers, we know what it is in its relation to performance on the stage.

Personality is all that you are in terms of your physical, mental and personal characteristics. It is the product of your physical endowments, plus your mental, emotional and spiritual development. It is the visible expression of yourself in manner and mannerisms. The dictionary says that it is your "distinction or excellence of personal and social traits, a magnetic personal quality, an integrated group of emotional trends, behavior tendencies, etc."

Thus it is evident that your personality as a singer is not something you have or you haven't. It is what you are. You don't have to be born with an attractive personality, but its quality can be cultivated, and it can be influenced by your will, and by your environment or life's circumstances or events.

If you are fortunate enough to inherit a healthy body, be sure to learn early its priceless value. Learn every possible means of preserving that health, whether it be by your philosophy of life or by physical care. More singing careers have been curtailed or ruined by physical inadequacies than by any other means.

I have spoken of *magnetism* as a radiation of health and good feeling. A healthy person feels good and shows it. A healthy person usually has a good disposition. Attitudes of cordiality and enthusiasm are easy for him. Whether adequate rest, diet or exercise are the best means of maintaining that effervescent kind of health, the singer will know best for himself.

Stage Deportment

Another phase of physical personality is expressed in stage deportment. We all appreciate the importance of good posture, but how about carriage? How do you walk? When you come upon the stage, do you stride or bounce or shuffle? If you are a woman do you walk with gliding grace, or do you plod or stride? While there is not sufficient space here to make suggestions, there is one point especially worth noting in stage deportment. Some people have good carriage coming onto the stage, but a very bad one going off. Make your stage walk a matter of observation, study and practice.

I am convinced that every singer who appears as a soloist in public should have the benefit of some kind of systematic body training. In previous generations every course of training for singers included dancing, fencing, eurythmics, or some other kind of formal physical exercise. Singers were expected to be actors or actresses. Every moment on the stage includes some kind of pantomime. Television, moving pictures, musical comedy; all these require body as well as vocal expression.

Today, modern dancing is as frequently found to be good body training for men as well as for women. Modelling and the study of Dramatic Art are also useful. In any case graceful carriage, and free expressive movement from head to toe, and from toe to head, is a part of the art of presentation.

How do you stand? I have seen people stand

148

beautifully—women poised like birds for flight, or men gracefully at ease. I have seen others whose feet seemed rooted to the ground like carrots. It is a part of stage deportment to handle the feet well.

How about gestures? Is your face free of any kind of grimace or any other kind of expression not related to what you are saying? Vocal efforts or personal attitudes have no right to intrude upon the attention of the audience. *The singer belongs to the song.* Facial expressions from any other source are evident in the tone color as well as in the appearance, so the peaceful countenance is as important in radio as it is on the stage.

What to do with the hands has long been a problem with the young or inexperienced singer. The answer is that we are seeking over-all poise. The hands should be as little in evidence as possible. The best advice is to let them alone. The less you are aware of them, the more likely you are to be free of any concern about them. Some people move too much and thus disconcert or distract the audience. Hands and feet should be quiet, not be moved about a great deal, but they should not be unnaturally set either.

How do you acknowledge applause? There is an effective manner of bowing for every type of figure, and for every occasion. In concert the end of a song calls for one kind of bow, while the end of a group of songs calls for a deeper bow and perhaps several repetitions of it. Stage bows when in costume allow much more extreme stage deportment. Study what best fits you and the occasion, and then practice before a mirror. It looks very amateurish to leave the manner of bowing to chance. It is a form of expression to the audience and a distinctive personality feature.

Good grooming should be taken for granted. For women the hairdo and the makeup may need professional advice. Men should avoid the odd or unusual in grooming or dress. There is a kind of dress appropriate to formal occasion, another for semi-formal and still another for informal or casual appearances. Good taste should be the infallible guide, so that we do not over-emphasize or under-estimate the importance of any point in physical appearance.

Personality Traits

But personality is something more than physical. It is a behavior pattern too. Everyone has seen how hereditary and environmental influences affect behavior. Which of the two kinds is stronger has never been settled to the satisfaction of all. In the broad sense hereditary influences such as race, nationality or type are inescapable. Environment plays an important part as well. But in the final analysis, personality is the sum total of what you are, spiritually, mentally and physically. But what you are is largely what you have become as a result of the life experiences you have had and the emotions and thoughts that govern your self-expression. This is the field in which you can exercise choice in behavior. You can seem radiant and luminous, or preoccupied and overly serious. You can give the impression that what you are doing is easy or that it is difficult. You can seem insecure, or give the impression that you have fully accepted yourself—and being convinced, prove yourself convincing. The behavior pattern runs an entire gamut of possibilities.

The most desirable personality to reflect is the one which seems victorious over the problems of life and work. A generous giver of himself and all that he is, is sure to win friends and influence people.

In addition to the attributes of physical endowment and of behavior, personality can be said to have an *aura*. The dictionary defines aura as a "distinctive atmosphere surrounding a person such as 'an aura of sanctity.' " We are surrounded by an aura that is instinctively sensed by those who see and hear us just as a flower is bathed in the scent of its own fragrance. We express this aura when we are perfectly still. People are aware of your background of feeling. An artist may have spent a lifetime of study and experience which aid in molding his personality; that *aura* or personality strikes the audience the moment he walks on the stage.

There are four major points by which impressarios, producers, conductors and concert managers seem to judge the acceptability of a singing artist. These are vocal technique, musicianship, diction, personality and appearance. My own experience as a singer and teacher has been that in judging a number of auditioners, those with the most attractive appearance or the most arresting personality are preferred. This does not mean that the other qualifications are minimized. But it does mean that personality seems to take first place in the minds of those who engage talent. This is probably correct from their point of view, because it is the first and most important criterion of judgment in the minds of the public. With voice, musicianship and diction present to

151

at least an acceptable degree, it is the personality that captures the interest.

How may the singer best develop an attractive personality. He may do so by selecting the most arresting personality he has observed and studying every activity of that individual. He should note the evident freedom and degree of feeling. He should observe the carriage and the manner in which clothes are worn. He should evaluate the evident mental attitude, and whether the artist is secure in his own feeling and confident of the efficacy of his preparation. The singer should notice whether the artist sings with the heart or only with the brain. He should examine the performer to find out if there is a warm appreciative response on the part of the audience and figure out why. He should observe whether mastery of all the details of the materials and the required technique have brought a feeling of complete self-acceptance and approval.

If you, as the singer, observe these things in the successful artist you would like to emulate, you have a useful guide to the development of your own personality as a public performer.

THE PSYCHOLOGICAL
ASPECT OF SUCCESS

THE VOICE IS A FUNCTIONAL INSTRUMENT; THERE-
fore, its action is automatic response to the con-
ceptual and executive capacities of the mind.
"Having a voice" is not merely a physical gift.
Many people have vigorous healthy bodies and exceptionally strong throats, yet these are of no use
for singing unless those same people are talented
musically, and have a clear sense of vocal sound.
Precisely this sense and this talent make the singer. The vocal mechanism, (the healthier and
stronger, the better) has no choice but to obey
the mental imagery, that fiat of will which paints
the best paintings, writes the best poetry, creates
the most beautiful sculpture and architecture, and
yes, writes the best books.

Even casual observation of the conspicuous fig-
ures in the worlds of art, science or business will
disclose that it is not always those who possess
some particular talent who occupy its high places.
Instead, it is those whose power is mental, who are
able to apply themselves intelligently to a given

task, and who untiringly work out every detail. Simplicity, directness, definiteness and absolute honesty are usually the characteristics of their thinking. Such minds scorn the vacillation, indecision, indifference and mental wanderings which characterize those who fail to reach the heights of achievement.

The Requirements of Success

It is no more difficult to succeed in the business of singing than in any other branch of human enterprise, if once its requirements are fully recognized and met. The laws of singing can be known as definitely as those of any other science.

Since, however, the singer's product is produced in terms of himself, his own body, mind and emotions, it becomes necessary for him to submit to discipline, training and development. He grows proportionately in voice, musicianship and artistry as he gains in self-mastery.

The requirements for success as a singer are a normally good healthy voice, an accurate musical ear, a sound body and a clear mind. These are the singer's raw materials, and in them he possesses no more and no less than did many of our great artists at the beginning of their careers.

"Tone has its origin in the mind." The mind of man is his great and only work room. It is a law of life that human capacities grow only through use. The mind has untold capacities for growth, since through observation and study it can draw on all the experience of mankind, and through imagination, on infinitude for its supply.

Having the mind as its source, the voice will express only what the mind is capable of conceiving. If the mind can grow in richness and fullness from year to year, by intelligent exercise, it follows that the voice may grow also, and by the same method.

Vocal growth is growth in tonal perception, and in tonal consciousness. The voice may improve in beauty and effectiveness, for vocal development implies mental, rather than merely physical advancement. A singer has grasped the first truth of vocal excellence, when he understands that the gift of song is mental, and that the singer's physical experiences are merely the reflection of his mental processes. He has laid hold upon the key that may unlock for him the great storehouse of vocal possibilities.

The Student's Responsibility

The student however should realize that it does not lie within the power of a teacher, or any other outside agency, to endow him with the ability to sing beautifully. He must spend himself for what he wants. He must give of himself in clear thinking, and intelligently directed action, if he would realize success as a singer.

The inference is obvious. Reason, judgement, decision, analysis, definite application and will power inevitably will carry the serious student toward the goal he covets. Ignorance, cloudy thinking, vacillation, mental digressions and lack of a well-established philosophy, together with an absence of systematic mental habits will, as inevitably, carry him down to defeat and oblivion.

Artistic vocal expression is the result of fine coordination of physical, mental and emotional action. The singer himself must establish the causes by which his results are to be achieved. In his work of training the mind and the body, he will discover that he has both strong and weak points. The embryo artist who finds himself weak in any of the elements of artistic expression will do well to set himself joyously to the task of strengthening them. He will do this rather than accept any weakness as inevitable.

Only the weak-minded yield to discouragement and look for sympathy from others. Since, then, the mind is the instrument given to us, by which we may reach the desired heights of achievement, let us look well to this instrument and make sure that it is in good working order.

Mental Efficiency

One writer tells us that the average man or woman is only five per cent efficient in the use of the five senses. It is also possible that we all possess latent mental powers, which if brought into full use would open for us the doors of success.

Are your powers of perception keen? If not, practice observation. Turn the white light of attention upon all that you observe. Five people witnessing an automobile accident have been known to give five different versions of the incident. Do you see what you look at? Develop the ability for keen perception if in the past you were unobservant.

Can you apply yourself? Practice holding yourself to fixed lines of action for set periods of time. Are you decisive? If not, practice making decisions. It does not matter whether all your decisions are correct or not, but it is important that you act definitely in the light of the best understanding you have, until better understanding develops. Too many voice students today are drifting, drifting on uncharted seas to no particular harbor. Choose a port and steer for it through fair weather or foul.

Have you reasoning power? Do you strive to understand the background for a given course of action; or do you move forward blindly? Every exercise, every song phrase had an objective. Do you strive to know what it is, and why? If you do, you will act in the light of your *own* understanding rather than blindly following another. Keep the mind always open for new truths. While every intelligent person has opinions, it is not wise to become so opinionated that one shuts the door to new truths.

Can you concentrate? Concentration is directed attention plus will. If you are weak in this, set yourself to the task of strengthening this faculty by definite exercise. Read Haddock's *Power of Will* for suggestions and exercises.

Do you exercise self-control? Do your moods control you, or do you control your moods? Do you allow a whole day to be wasted because you are not in the proper mood for study? Or, do you allow discouragement to numb your faculties and retard your progress? Then practice mental selection. Think what you choose to think, and choose what your higher self knows to be beneficial to you. It is encouraging to remember that by changing negative thinking to positive thinking and destructive thinking to constructive thinking, you can change the conditions and circumstances of your life. It is a certain sign of weakness if you allow yourself to be governed entirely by outside and uncontrollable circumstances.

Have you will power? Nature supplies us with a reserve energy which will appear whenever it is required, and give that added degree of power necessary to conquer a difficulty. Resolve upon a wise course of action, and then follow it with the power made possible by this reserve force. The will is the majestic faculty, holding supremacy over all the others. Therefore, cultivate will in terms of positive, constructive action.

It must now be evident that the great need of students is for clear thinking and avoidance of indefinite and negative states of mind. Exercise selection and constantly act with the thought of the future ever present. Even a commonplace and monotonous task grows in interest to the point of fascination when it is viewed in the light of its desired end. Strive to eliminate mental carelessness, indifference, prejudice and scattered thinking. Make it your constant purpose to secure definite working ideas; then go to work upon them.

I think too, that the imperative need, in the mental processes of voice students, is order. There are rich rewards for you if you will but be certain that your thinking is concise and orderly. Think in a straight line to your goal, and allow no counter attraction to interrupt the direction of endeavor or divert attention from your objective. In your next practice period, make a note of your practice habits. Observe how your mind works. Does your mind wander? Have you fallen into set habits? Or do you systematically pass from subject to subject, working out the details singly, and always with the basic and guiding principles in mind? We know that many factors enter into a practice period. There are breathing, intonation, vowels, consonants, range, dynamics, color, flexibility, agility, enthusiasm, memory and imagination. Do you classify them and work them in order? Do you select the weak points and call forth your reserve power to strengthen them? And do you avoid the time wasting distractions of chatting with friends complaining about the weather, the accompaniment, the work involved, and a 1001 other deterrents to achievement?

Earlier in the chapter, the writer referred to the teacher as only one of several sources from which the student could draw inspiration and materials for his advancement. Surely it is of first importance to the student to determine what his sources are, and then to set himself to draw upon them.

Briefly, the singer's guides are these:

First, always, his lessons with a reliable teacher.

Second, observation. That is observation of the lives, habits, and more important still, the work of the great artists of his profession. No singer can grow without worthy models to furnish materials for his imagination. Hearing great artists is absolutely essential to growth as singers.

Third, reading. This applies to all good literature, of course, but more particularly to history, drama, poetry, and with discrimination, works upon the voice.

Fourth, listening; not just hearing, but *listening* critically to great performances. Among the areas of listening are great artists of all kinds, orchestras, operas and dramas.

Fifth, life itself, the school of humanity, for singing to be of value must have human appeal. A deep sympathy, a love for all humanity, a wide horizon, and a zest for life are all vitally necessary to the artist who would strike the universal note.

The sensitive singer, keeping his mind alert,

will miss no opportunity to enrich his store of material. There is no other method by which all the material thus acquired can enlarge the personal ability of the artist, except the formula of work. It is the only magic word in the profession. The gap between knowledge and realization can be bridged only by work, for through work capacity is developed.

The efforts, however, must be unhampered by faulty mental machinery. No point must be left obscured. The singer should ask questions, be thorough, and use calm judgment. He should avoid emotional states of self-pity and moody aberrations of mind. He must spend his energy in achieving, without distractions of any type, the goal he most desires.

If he has patience, and in the meantime works diligently, he will soon feel power coming to him, power by which he may achieve convincing, effective performance.

THE CAREER

THE SINGING ARTIST MUST KNOW NOT ONLY HOW
to sing, but also how to make his singing pay. This
chapter deals with singing as a career. The singer's situation—where he lives, whom he knows,
how he is situated in life—is different from that of
others; but, nevertheless, he will find value in
certain general principles.

I take for granted that he understands the
importance of a musical education and the capacity to convey idea and feeling through the medium
of language. Because his voice is important, it
should be adequately trained for the type of
music he intends to sing.

There is no substitute for talent and skill. The
first requirement for success is *excellence*. The
singer must be really good at something. Perhaps
he has a beautiful voice, artistry, an extensive repertoire and a developed technique; or his special
quality may be personal charm, with good looks,
authority and sincerity of expression; maybe his
innate musicality and attractive manner make a

direct appeal to the music lover. He must have *something* that has risen above the commonplace and ordinary. And yet his qualities must be sufficiently balanced so that nothing is conspicuously missing.

By the time a singer goes "into business" he knows what his assets are, and will emphasize them accordingly. He knows his limitations, too, and will work faithfully to overcome them so that he will advance to higher levels on an ever widening front.

In the past three or four decades the entertainment field has received new emphasis. The limitations imposed by undeveloped broadcasting mediums, inadequate microphones and speakers made music produced at high frequency levels undesirable. The medium was limited in its capacity.

As this is written in 1957 these mechanisms have been greatly improved. The faithful recording of famous singing artists is now possible. But in the meantime, the limited medium brought in a new custom of broadcasting and recording the female voice.

To avoid the "blasting" effect, female voices were required to sing much lower in pitch so that their voices were on the same frequency level as the male voice. This made necessary the elimination of all vibrato, which, as every acoustician knows, is the secret of the natural quality or the beauty of the female voice.

There entered then the *straight tone* described as a cold, hard sound, as opposed to a *legitimate* tone which was not tolerated. These terms are those of the broadcasting and show businesses and are not my own.

As a result, singers of popular songs disregarded vocal and musical standards in favor of *style* and *delivery*. The delivery technique is based on diction and personality. There must be *appeal* or, as one of them put it, "I must sound sexy and intimate."

Thus a new standard appears in which sentiment is rated above sincere feeling and jingles above poetry. This is claimed to be the music of youth and romance, but it is the idealized illusion of the teen-agers, rather than the expression of anything that could be called a culture.

It must be music that can be danced to, therefore the constant (even monotonous) repetition of a rhythmic *beat* is its chief characteristic. Appreciation of it requires no education. Its appeal lies in the fact that it is a diversion, an escape mechanism by which the circumstances and obligations of daily life are momentarily forgotten.

There are many successful people in show business, but they violate all the principles of good singing, good music and pure understandable English. They are personalities, stylized, and in many cases husky-throated crooners or shouters who "belt out a song" much to the amusement of those who come to be entertained.

Enthusiasm, eccentricity or dramatic talent take the place of music and poetry and those who prefer true music are "squares" to the pseudo-sophisticates. Popular music as it is sold today is for the young. Both its performers and its listeners must be either extremely youthful or culturally undeveloped.

I do not agree with Mr. Charles Henderson who says in his book *How to Sing for Money*,

"If the money opportunities for singers were in the classical field, I'd be writing about

163

classical songs. But they aren't. The quickest and biggest money today for trained singers as well as the beginner is in the effective singing of popular songs. You are in the business of furnishing entertainment. Boldly, to get money from your customers, the listening public, you must give them what they want."

Do the singers of popular music really find a more ready market for their wares than the accomplished musician? They do if we are willing to concede that they work long hours every day of the week for extended periods for wages rather than for fees.

The singer who can project an attractive personality effectively is more nearly an actor or actress than a singing artist. All musical values attached to real music as it has evolved through past centuries have been minimized to practical extinction by so-called popular music.

Even with the rising crescendo of press agentry, promotion, production and managerial maneuvering, the true artist can still command a fee for a single performance that exceeds the weekly fees of most night club entertainers who must work from 9:00 p.m. to 4:00 a.m. or thereabouts, six or seven days a week.

The best popular song singer is at heart an actor, and as his voice ages, he usually turns to a dramatic career. Some have made this transition so successfully that they have won *Oscars* in the moving picture world. They have learned the value of hard work and thorough preparation. They deplore, among others, the "trash music" of the present day.

Good music represents the culture of an era,

not a "here-today, gone-tomorrow" type. It will survive the clamor of press agents and publicity mediums, as well as the ruinous effect of "popularity."

In the end it is the total response of a well-integrated personality that determines the worth of a public performer rather than some single factor. And the performer will guard against being a mere "flash in the pan" if he keeps working to excel in serious music, besides whatever he is doing locally and temporarily.

In the entertainment field competition is tremendous. But the public's hunger for the really fine artist-singer is never satisfied. There is a distinction between the singing artist and the entertainer. Both fields have much value, but there is considerable difference between them.

The true music lover wants something that satisfies his soul and complements his intellect. The music of the masters is just as alive today as when it was written, for it contains the essence of immortality. The artist who brings this to an educated public is honored and loved. Both the artist and his music never lose their appeal, but the appeal is one that satisfies both the intellect and the soul's hunger for truly great and artistic accomplishment.

Many an ambitious young artist is asking himself, "What must I *do* to interest people?" What is that "plus quality" which singles one person out at an audition, and sends the rest home with a polite "thank you"?

When the chorus parts for *South Pacific* were cast, hundreds of young singers, for three full days, filled the alley leading to the stage entrance of the Majestic Theater in New York. They were waiting to be auditioned. The management let them in ten at a time, and about one in ten was given an opportunity to sing or answer questions about himself.

This is not said to discourage anyone, but to illustrate the seriousness of the competition in such booking centers as New York or Hollywood. To be discouraged is to be without courage, and courage (the kind that is meant when we speak of "the courage of one's conviction") is a basic requirement in any competitive field. I know at least a dozen people who were in that alley who are prosperous today. Most of them were well trained singers. When Grace Moore went to New York, her first engagement was in a night club. The next was in a musical comedy called *Hitchy-Koo*. After that she sang the songs of Irving Berlin for three seasons in the *Music Box Revue*. Her operatic training came later, and few have surpassed her "Mimi" and "Louise."

The cynical statement, "It's not what you can do, it's whom you know," is, happily, usually untrue. The day of buying one's way into acceptance is over. Now agencies, managements, producers, engagers of all talent are convinced that the final arbiter is the public.

There is much difference of opinion about what the public wants, but if an artist has something the public does want, his opportunities will come as soon as he is really ready, but not before.

The demands of the performing field are severe, but only because the public is a severe impersonal judge. It does not take into account that one may need money, or that he must prove himself by a certain time. Neither does it let him set his own standards. It sets them for him. People may reject the attributes of one artist but accept the same qualities in another. He is an individual, but the public sees him as a type and quickly senses whether what he is doing is appropriate to his type and talents or not. This rule holds if he auditions for a night club, an opera company, or any other musical activity.

He should observe, watch and listen to those who do succeed. Find out why, and in finding out, he should never listen to gossip. For the one who succeeds because of favoritism, there are dozens who have won recognition by merit alone.

Career Advice

My advice to the young singer is: Conquer the ground upon which you stand. Are you a success in your own city? The magic word behind all success is experience. "But," you say, "how can I gain experience when I am not given the opportunity to sing?" This is the constant dilemma of the ambitious artist. You can't sing successfully in opera without having sung in opera. Concert managements demand that you be a proven artist with box office appeal before they will book you. You can't get a recording company to cut a record, nor an agent to handle your affairs until you have a history of successful public performances. But singers with initiative, ingenuity and a willingness to gain experience wherever they can are coming to public attention constantly. There is always some way to gain experience in your chosen field if you have faith in yourself and are willing to do whatever you must do to gain proper perspective.

If you are not a local success, why not? You can find out if you try. It is not important that you agree with all your critics, but if you made a certain kind of impression that is in any way inadequate or unfavorable, there is nothing to prevent your trying to improve. If your motive is a deep desire to express yourself in music, and you place that desire first in your life, there is no reason why you cannot succeed. Perhaps you need some avenue of specialization. Many singers find playing in summer theaters a great help. Others, not content with a merely conventional musical education, have become expert sight readers and have made a good income in ensembles and small choral groups, while others specialized in some other field suggested by their own talents. In any case, specialization is a distinct advantage.

Television

Television is a rapidly growing medium. Singers in training are advised to watch themselves in full length mirrors and to listen to recordings of their singing. It is not reasonable to expect the public to look at, listen to, and pay for what you are not willing to face yourself. Television is an intimate medium. Your audiences sit only a few feet from your image on the screen. They can increase the volume at will. Singing on television and on the radio, in moving pictures and on records presents all the problems of mass production.

You must know yourself. Who you are and what you are, and you should not hesitate to give of yourself even though doing so reveals your very soul. Have you followed the great rule, *Man, know thyself?*

In this country beautiful voices are plentiful, but people who know *what to do* when they sing

168

are rare. Mr. Goldofsky of the Metropolitan Opera and Boston University made an interesting statement not long ago. He said, "Surely faces were meant to express something besides tone production."

How do you think most singers' faces look when they sing? Are their thoughts on themselves, or on what they are talking about? Do eyes, facial expressions and body movements belong to the singing? They should; every part of the singer's body should reflect the mood and theme of the music.

There is more. Managers, agents and producers do not come to your house and ring the doorbell. You must go to them. Do you do that? Do the people who engage talent know you? Do you know who they are? When you do go to them, do you follow every lead? A very successful radio singer that I know had ten to twelve radio auditions at the same station. Each time she was rebuffed. Each time she came back saying, "I have improved since last time. See how you like this." Never take "no" for a final answer. Ask for criticism, ask for suggestions, and you will get them. Then act on them. Say, "They will never say that about me again."

In the early stages of your career, do not quibble about price. Take any opportunity to sing and do not despise nor avoid small beginnings, for it is experience you need. On the other hand, if a radio program or a church position is known to have certain value, expect to be paid accordingly. Marian Anderson sang in a church in Philadelphia and often for nothing. She did this for a number of years while studying the best in vocal literature. Then, when Koussevitsky heard her, she was ready. A choral conductor recently auditioned several young singers. When he was asked afterwards what his impressions were, he said, "Very good. They sing very well, and will sing those oratorios well, when they have lived with them for a while." Until a song or a role is "sung in," until it has become a part of the singer's being, the audience feels that he is not fully prepared, and the critics soon say so. There is no substitute for experience.

Summary of Vocal Fields

A quick review of the various fields of activity or outlets for a singer's services might be in order. First, there is the "noble road." A person with a fine voice, well trained and under complete control, and who has also become an accomplished musician and an adequate linguist is on this road to acceptance and success.

Considerable preparation in repertoire, both in classic and modern song, and experience in singing with an orchestra, especially for oratorio or radio, must then be added.

This kind of background combined with attractive appearance, communicative interpretation and social grace, should result in a remunerative career.

In this country opportunities in opera usually follow, rather than precede these qualifications.

For many, the first step is singing in a church. A church job affords not only a steady income, however small or large, but also a constantly repeated opportunity for practical experience. The church job leads naturally to oratorio. Oratorio engagements are occasional, and while rarely a living in themselves, help to increase the annual income.

Singers are often called upon to direct choirs or choral societies. Here the thoroughness of the music'l education becomes important as well as the capacity to conduct, which is not difficult to acquire. But more important is the fact that conducting develops the capacity for leadership and the ability to handle people. Both of these considerations are primary in the business of singing.

Some will turn to the stage. A job in the chorus of an opera company or a musical comedy company pays well. The amount is determined by such organizations as Equity or a union. Night club work also has income rates determined by unions, as does radio. Principal or solo roles come after experience has been acquired or special abilities have been revealed.

Some with college musical educations enter the teaching field in high schools, universities or private teaching.

Ensemble Singing

Singing in ensemble is an important and often neglected way of getting into the business. Trios, duos and quartets obtain engagements more easily than solos. These jobs are often secured from clubs, occasional concerts, television and radio. Singing in groups is good ear training and improves the ability to read music and to sing with others as one must do on the stage.

Contests

Contests and competitions offer opportunities for recognition as well as for prizes. Those who do

171

not have the moral courage to face competition should be reminded that every important engagement is obtained through audition. Auditions are contests. You may as well learn the psychology of competition early. Important assignments come after there is artistic maturity. Of course, it must be born in mind we are speaking of "good music."

In the entertainment field of popular music anything goes and often does. One will become famous because he cries when he sings, but it must be done with conviction in such a fashion as to arouse compassion and not amusement in the audience. Such careers are short. Another is recognized because of personal beauty, a "sexy" voice, or such a thing as extreme youth which is also a novelty. Sometimes, however, a singer in the entertainment field "sends" people and is therefore accepted. Usually such an experience is based on an innate acting ability. In any case communicative intimacy must not be underestimated. Singing in concerts and in solo spots on radio is done by so-called "name singers." They are the people who have become known through frequent appearances over a long period of time, or who have gained recognition through some fortuitous circumstances. Often they are opera singers or have gained recognition because they belong to an opera company.

In all the relations a singer might have with directors, agents, or producers, he must quickly gain a reputation for dependability. His word must be good. He must be punctual in keeping his appointments. He must be discreet, particularly in what he says about other singers or those who employ him. He must have mastered all of the details of attractive public appearance, and must have the poise and the *inner emotional control* that enables him to face a microphone, an audience, or audition and still be at his best.

In the long run, a self-dedicated person who sings for the love of singing, who strives for perfection, who is single in purpose, and who puts singing first in his life's program, not second or third or fourth in terms of time, money, and creative thinking, is the one who finally arrives and wins a lasting place in whatever branch of the art his talent deserves.

Public Relations for the Singer

Every new singer faces the problem of becoming known to the public. A singer must learn how to use publicity media wisely. He can waste money by not advertising enough, by advertising too much, and also by advertising before he has anything to advertise. Therefore, strive to deserve and obtain favorable press publicity and use such notices in your own printed circulars or brochures. Then build up a mailing list of the kind of people you want to approach. Have your brochures include an attractive photograph of yourself. Do not be discouraged if the benefits are slow in coming. I have known of singers with bushels of press notices, and yet managers insisted they had never heard of them. To obtain good publicity is a problem requiring study.

Singing for Pleasure

There is plenty of justification for those who sing just for pleasure, to improve themselves and to give pleasure to others. To such it is an avocation at least as pleasant as photography, golf, or any other hobby. There are many who make such an avocation pay well.

In any event, life satisfaction, doing what you want to do and exercising the creative faculties, is always richly rewarding.

Finally the young American singer, aiming at a career in the performing field, must be prepared to be versatile. A large radio or television station which offers the new singer an opportunity to be heard from coast to coast requests that its auditioners bring an operatic aria, a light classic and a popular song. Light classics are songs from stage productions such as *Oklahoma, Vagabond King, Desert Song* and *South Pacific* while the popular songs are the dance arrangements of the day.

While these requirements offend the artistic tastes of discriminating musicians, it must be remembered that opportunity for recognition comes first. Choice of a specific field comes afterward. The singer trained in serious music should take the attitude that he or she can do anything that popular song singers can do. Several of our best known opera stars are proving this on radio and television right now.

We may as well recognize that the conversational informality, the intimacy and the sentimentality of popular songs have made them the folk music of America, without for a moment threatening the lasting supremacy of the music of the masters.